Her Freedom Journey

Her Freedom Journey

A GUIDE OUT OF PORN & SHAME TO AUTHENTIC INTIMACY

dr. Juli Slattery & dr. Joy Skarka

MOODY PUBLISHERS

CHICAGO

All Scripture quotations, unless otherwise indicated, are taken from the Holy Bible, New International Version®, NIV®. Copyright ©1973, 1978, 1984, 2011 by Biblica, Inc.™ Used by permission of Zondervan. All rights reserved worldwide. www.zondervan.com The "NIV" and "New International Version" are trademarks registered in the United States Patent and Trademark Office by Biblica, Inc.™

Scripture quotations marked (ESV) are from the ESV® Bible (The Holy Bible, English Standard Version®), © 2001 by Crossway, a publishing ministry of Good News Publishers. Used by permission. All rights reserved. The ESV text may not be quoted in any publication made available to the public by a Creative Commons license. The ESV may not be translated in whole or in part into any other language.

Scripture quotations marked (NLT) are taken from the Holy Bible, New Living Translation, copyright ©1996, 2004, 2015 by Tyndale House Foundation. Used by permission of Tyndale House Publishers, Carol Stream, Illinois 60188. All rights reserved.

All emphasis in Scripture has been added.

Names and details of some stories have been changed to protect the privacy of individuals.

Some content has been previously published in the authors' books and on their blogs at authenticintimacy.com and joyskarka.com.

Published in association with Wolgemuth & Wilson.

Edited by Amanda Cleary Eastep
Interior design: Puckett Smartt
Cover design: Brittany Schrock
Author photo, Slattery: The Cannons Photography
Author photo, Skarka: Shy Quiles

Library of Congress Cataloging-in-Publication Data

Names: Slattery, Julianna, 1969- author. | Skarka, Joy, author.
Title: Her freedom journey : a guide out of porn and shame to authentic
   intimacy / Dr. Juli Slattery and Dr. Joy Skarka.
Description: Chicago, IL : Moody Publishers, 2024. | Includes
   bibliographical references. | Summary: "Our prayer is that through this
   book you would better understand God's love and through that love, you
   will begin your journey of healing and freedom!"– Provided by
   publisher.
Identifiers: LCCN 2023056828 (print) | LCCN 2023056829 (ebook) | ISBN
   9780802432704 (paperback) | ISBN 9780802472786 (ebook)
Subjects: LCSH: Pornography–Religious aspects–Christianity. |
   Women–Sexual behavior. | Sex addiction–Religious
   aspects–Christianity. | Integrity–Religious aspects–Christianity. |
   Intimacy (Psychology)–Religious aspects–Christianity. | BISAC:
   RELIGION / Christian Living / Women's Interests | SELF-HELP / Compulsive
   Behavior / Sex & Pornography Addiction
Classification: LCC BV4597.6 .S57 2024 (print) | LCC BV4597.6 (ebook) |
   DDC 241.6/67–dc23/eng/20240224
LC record available at https://lccn.loc.gov/2023056828
LC ebook record available at https://lccn.loc.gov/2023056829

Originally delivered by fleets of horse-drawn wagons, the affordable paperbacks from D. L. Moody's publishing house resourced the church and served everyday people. Now, after more than 125 years of publishing and ministry, Moody Publishers' mission remains the same—even if our delivery systems have changed a bit. For more information on other books (and resources) created from a biblical perspective, go to www.moodypublishers.com or write to:

Moody Publishers
820 N. LaSalle Boulevard
Chicago, IL 60610

1 3 5 7 9 10 8 6 4 2

Printed in the United States of America

To the Authentic Intimacy community: Your passion, commitment, and vulnerability have given us the courage to create this book. May the Lord continue to set His people free from sexual sin, bondage, and brokenness!

Contents

Meet the Authors:
An Introduction to This Book

From Joy:

I opened my door and there she stood. I invited Anna inside my home and offered her a cup of coffee. As we sat down on my couch, I could see her hesitancy and the shame on her face as she could barely make eye contact with me. She began to tell me a bit of her story.

She cried as she confessed her porn addiction for the first time. "When I was in middle school, my friend introduced me to porn. I continued looking at it out of curiosity, but it quickly became an addiction. Now, years later, I'm questioning if I will ever find freedom and if God still loves me."

I have met with countless women like Anna. They love the Lord but can't seem to shake the temptation and shame of sexual sin. They have different types of trauma, struggles, and brokenness, but their questions have a familiar ring:

"Will I ever be free from porn?"

"Will my life always feel this empty?"

"Would anyone really love me if they knew?"

"Can Jesus really meet my longings and desires for intimacy?"

Not long ago, I was the woman asking these questions, only I had no safe place to voice them. I felt empty, shameful, worthless, and lonely. After nights of endless scrolling and watching videos that I knew I shouldn't watch, I questioned how God could love me. Feeling lonely, isolated, and alienated from God, I would turn back to porn for comfort. Maybe, just like me, your struggle with sexual sin causes you to doubt God's love for you. You are not alone.

I haven't always shared my story openly with others. In the past, I often feared that people would reject me. The first time I publicly shared my story of sexual addiction to pornography, someone said to me, "Do you want to be known as the *porn girl*?" Immediately, I regretted sharing the intimate details of my life with strangers. For years, I believed this lie that I was "porn girl," until my boyfriend (now husband) changed my perspective when he said, "You're not porn girl. You're *freedom* girl."

You are not alone in this struggle—I have been there. I know how difficult it is to pick up a book like this one! I've been stuck in the cycle of sexual sin and shame, and now I'm living in freedom. This doesn't mean my story is wrapped up in a bow (there are days when I'm still tempted or triggered), but it does mean I'm closer to understanding godly sexuality. We're on this journey together to become more like Christ, grow in our understanding of sexual wholeness and integrity, and to discover authentic intimacy.

I also want to give you a heads-up. Throughout the book I'm going to honestly share pieces of my story that might be triggering for you. I'm sharing in order to help bring hope and healing and so you know that you're not alone. I never include graphic details, but if anything feels too heavy, feel free to pause and come back to the book at another time. We also encourage you to talk through any unhealed trauma with a licensed professional counselor.

From Juli:

In 2012, God called me to start a ministry called Authentic Intimacy. With training and experience as a Christian psychologist, I was somewhat familiar with typical questions women asked about sexuality, shame, and longings. Yet, the Lord opened my heart in a new way to really *see* the women around me. So many of them carried unanswered questions and unspoken shame around sexuality. Married and unmarried, young and old, God's women were suffering.

A few years into ministering to women specifically on topics of sexual brokenness, I began to realize that we are all sexually broken. I began to see my own sexual brokenness and identify with women with whom I once thought I had nothing in common. Not every woman struggles with pornography, but every woman has had the beautiful gift of sexuality tainted in some way by lust, assault, legalism, betrayal, or exposure to sexual experiences and images their brains and hearts could not process.

I have learned that sexual freedom comes through the process of discipleship—the intentional pursuit of an intimate relationship with God. The Lord could zap you and make all of your painful memories and tempting thoughts vanish. I think we all sometimes wish He would do that! But God in His wisdom (which is often nothing like our wisdom) has chosen to change us day by day, as we learn to surrender more of ourselves to Him.

MAKING THE MOST OF THIS GUIDE

This is not just a book; it is an invitation to go deeper with the Lord. Each of the eight weeks includes four days of teaching with personal reflection questions and challenges. You'll discover practical tools for your freedom journey, and you will experience the love of God more intimately as you read His Word. We will

The spiritual battle around your sexuality is real.

frequently encourage you to turn to Scripture, so have a Bible nearby in order to read God's Word as you go through the book.

You can journey through this book by yourself or with a group. Discuss your thoughts with a friend to create accountability and experience freedom from shame. In a group setting, make sure to read the whole week and spend time processing and writing down answers to the discussion questions on your own before your group meets.

You may find that temptation actually increases as you go through this book. Don't let that surprise you. The spiritual battle around your sexuality is real. The enemy does not want you to experience freedom and really doesn't want you to have a deeper relationship with God. He might stomp his feet by accusing you, discouraging you, and telling you the lie that there is no hope. Don't believe him. Just keep showing up.

Right now, you might feel defeated. You might doubt that Jesus can meet your needs and heal your wounds. Maybe you are hesitant to start this book because you've tried everything and are afraid to hope. Jesus died to give you freedom. Jesus calls you "daughter" and desires you to know that you are loved, wanted, and cherished. You might ask, "What if I get to the end of this book and I still struggle?" Remember this is one step on your freedom journey toward authentic intimacy.

As you're going through this resource, you might want to dig deeper into an issue you're currently struggling with, like recovering from abuse or finding healing in your marriage. This book is just one resource from the ministry Authentic Intimacy. At authenticintimacy. com, you will find blogs, podcasts, and much more to help you learn more about specific areas of sexuality.

We want to encourage you for taking this step toward healing and freedom. You may hit roadblocks, but in those moments, remember three things . . .

You are LOVED.
You are not alone.
We are praying with you.

Joy and Juli

The Problem of Porn

I (Joy) remember how my voice trembled as I barely gathered the courage to say the words, "I'm struggling with watching porn," to my mentor over coffee.

Do you know what gave me that courage? Someone else went first. I heard a courageous woman share her story at a college student women's event. Until that moment, I had never heard a woman admit that she struggled with sexual sin. I can still picture the event. Thirty college students all crammed into a living room, listening to every word of this brave woman sharing her story.

For the first time, I realized I wasn't alone and that I wasn't a total freak for being a woman who struggled with sexual sin.

In all my time in the church, I'd rarely heard someone talk about sexual struggles, and I had never heard a woman confess porn use. When I've heard Christian leaders address sexual struggle and temptation, they do so as if it's only a man's issue. This makes women who are struggling with porn, habitual masturbation, or other unwanted sexual desires feel even more shame. I honestly thought something might be wrong with me. What I've learned since then is that women struggle too!

More than one out of three visitors to adult sites are women, and this number grows each year.[1] In my doctoral research, I surveyed over one thousand Christian women. Sixty-nine percent of the women felt far from God because of their sexual shame surrounding their sexual sin, and 52 percent lived a secret life, hiding their sexual sin from others.[2] Thirty percent of the women surveyed shared they felt sexual shame because of their struggles with pornography and compulsive masturbation.[3] These statistics show that you are not alone. Sadly, many women struggle in secret.

Women all around you are carrying similar struggles and shame. When we all remain silent, no one finds the freedom to step into the light. I'm so grateful that someone went first, giving me the permission and courage to be honest. Now I want to "go first" for you!

Why Porn Is a Problem

I (Joy) first saw porn in fifth grade. My friend and I returned from summer camp and went up to my room to play. I had a small laptop sitting on my desk and my friend said, "Let me show you something." She pulled up images of things I had never seen before—I had no idea what pornography was. In the moment, my heart began to race and I felt a tingling in my body. These feelings made me question if we should be looking at the images. I quickly turned my back, shutting my bedroom door so my parents wouldn't know what we were doing. After this incident, I wouldn't look at porn again until college, but it awakened my sexual desires and curiosities.

In college, I turned back to porn as a form of education—I had questions about sex and no safe person to ask. What started out as curiosity quickly turned into a coping mechanism when I felt sad or lonely. Because I never heard anyone talk about porn being an issue, especially for women, I thought, "What's the big deal with porn? At least I'm not sleeping around."

These are common thoughts for many women who don't see why porn is a problem. Pornography, hooking up, sexting, and other forms of sexual experimentation are a normal part of being a teen or young adult in today's world. So is it really a big deal if you look at pornography to address your pain, loneliness, and boredom?

We are writing this book from the perspective of two women who love God. We believe that He created sexual desire for a purpose, and that pornography is one way that we learn to misuse the gift of sex. Throughout our time together, you will see us return to this truth: your freedom journey happens when you find freedom from sin, shame, and bondage in a relationship with Jesus Christ.

Pornography is so common in our world today that we can't even imagine what life might be like without it. In some ways, porn affects us even when we are not looking at it. Today, we are going to look at three of the biggest ways porn hurts us. What you are going to read probably won't surprise you, but it may remind you that pornography acts as a thief, sneaking in and stealing something precious. As you read this, the purpose is not to pile on shame, but to highlight the importance of your freedom journey. We are starting with the *bad news* about pornography, but we promise we won't stay there.

PORN KEEPS US FROM OUR DEEPER LONGINGS

Imagine going to the doctor and hearing the alarming news that you are seriously malnourished. Your blood work shows that your body has not been getting the iron, calcium, and vitamins it needs to be healthy. In shock, you tell the doctor, "I don't understand! I never miss a meal!"

When the doctor asks you about your diet, you tell him that you eat the same thing every day: two donuts for breakfast, a hot dog and French fries for lunch, and a big plate of nachos and cookies for dinner. What's the problem? Your food has no nutritional value. These manufactured foods with high levels of sugar and fat keep you feeling too full for you to ever crave healthy food.

You were not created for sex; you were created for intimacy.

Porn works a lot like this. You have a natural desire for intimacy. You also have the natural ability to awaken sexual desire and enjoy sex within the committed relationship of marriage. Porn portrays fake intimacy, while God and community provide authentic intimacy. Porn shortcuts this natural desire and feeds you unnatural, manufactured pleasure. You were not created for sex; you were created for intimacy. You may be sexually acting out every day, but you are "malnourished" when it comes to intimacy.

Have you ever been surrounded by people but have felt alone and unknown? When I (Joy) was secretly struggling with porn, I would leave social events with friends and go home to watch porn. I thought porn would fix my longings and desires, but what I really needed was deep friendships and authentic community. Friends who knew my struggle, yet loved me. Friends who could point me back to God and encourage me in my healing journey. I was "malnourished" in my earthly relationships and in my relationship with God, yet I was looking to porn to fill my emptiness. At the end of the day, porn didn't cure my problems—I felt even emptier than before.

Describe a time when porn or hooking up made you feel even emptier.

Read Isaiah 55:1–2. List some of the ways you have "spent money on bread that doesn't satisfy."

PORN SEPARATES US FROM GOD

As you will learn throughout this book, God has a very specific design and intent for your sexuality. Choosing to look at porn or sleep around is choosing to do what we want instead of seeking God for our comfort and fulfillment. While there are many reasons why you might turn to porn, you can't get around the fact that using pornography is sin. It's a choice to do things your own way rather than turning to God.

Daily, we make small choices that can either lead us to God or away from God. Our decisions can bring us closer to Him, like spending time with Him or going to a community group. Or our choices can separate us from Him and pull us further into sin. For me (Joy), those wrong choices felt so small, but they added up over time. Choosing to watch certain shows or follow certain people on social media didn't hurt me at first, but seeing them over and over again negatively formed my desires. I was being sexually discipled by what I was watching, and that led my heart closer to porn than to God. I was choosing to walk in darkness just by the small choices I made.

My struggle with porn didn't start out this way, but I got to a point where I *wanted* to look at it. As hard as it is to say this, I desired porn and the rush and release of endorphins it brought me.

Read 1 John 1:5–10. How would you describe the difference between walking in "light" and walking in "darkness"?

Based on this passage, how does sexual sin keep you from a close relationship with God and other people?

What does this passage promise will happen if we confess our sins?

PORN TREATS PEOPLE LIKE OBJECTS

Porn impacts not just the way you think about sex, but how you view people. When we engage in porn, we are feeding a culture of selfishness. Porn trains you to approach sex with a selfish perspective. It gives you what you want when you want it. Intimacy (sexual, or any kind of intimacy) is the exact opposite. To build an intimate relationship, you have to approach the other person with the sensitivity and self-control to understand and address their needs.

Porn teaches you to *consume*. While consuming pornography, you take what you want. **Intimacy requires you to *connect***—to take intentional steps toward vulnerability, risk, and unselfish love. Sometimes couples say that they watch porn to learn how to "spice things up." Porn and erotica (literature written to sexually arouse the reader and sometimes referred to as soft porn because it is less graphic than porn) actually do the exact opposite. Maybe at first things will "spice up," but consuming porn and erotica will eventually erode the trust and communication needed for a loving and fulfilling sex life.

How has porn taught you to consume rather than connect?

In what ways do you think pornography in general is influencing the culture around you?

That's the bad news. But the good news is this: not only can you be set free, but God wants to heal and redeem the gifts porn has stolen from you!

Tomorrow, I (Joy) will share more of my story, but I can tell you the ending now: God healed and redeemed everything that porn stole from me. I'm living proof that healing is possible. Right now you might have trouble believing this for your own life, but I pray that by the end of this book your faith will grow as you watch miracles happen.

Why Porn Isn't Your Biggest Problem

*Trigger warning: this next section contains mention of sexual assault.

Night after night, I scrolled through porn on my phone. Images flickered across my screen, but they always left me longing for more. One image or video was never enough to rid my loneliness or cure my sexual desire. Just like a drug addiction, one hit never satisfied me. Over time, I needed harder porn and more variety. I thought porn was my biggest problem. It turns out this wasn't true. It was a problem in my life, but it was a symptom of a larger problem. Porn was my way to cope and numb the pain and loneliness I felt every day because of the sexual assault I experienced in college.[4]

Entering college, I longed to be loved. At my college orientation day, I met a guy and was date-raped that night. My body was taken, and I was left exposed. Depressed and filled with shame, I began to question God. Did He care? Why did He let this happen? Was it my fault? I had so many questions. I struggled with blaming myself, even though it was not my fault.

If you've been abused or experienced rape, I am so sorry. I know the emotional pain that is attached to sexual trauma. The sexual abuse you experienced was not your fault. Read this line again—it was not your fault. This truth is so hard to believe for those of us who have been abused.

After being date-raped on my third day of college, I quickly turned to porn to: 1) ask questions about sex, and 2) find comfort from the trauma. The pain from that rape dramatically changed my life. I went from being a student with As and Bs in high school to having to withdraw from a college class. Instead of being a social butterfly, I stayed in my dorm room, watching porn to escape from the emotional weight of the sexual trauma.

When I doubted that any man would love me once he heard my story, I turned to porn.

When sadness was the only emotion I could feel and I just wanted to feel an ounce of pleasure, I turned to the only comforter I knew: porn. Porn never provided lasting pleasure, comfort, or hope. I felt sneaky and dirty—hiding away in my college apartment while my roommate slept in the room next door or looking at screens in the middle of the night when I couldn't sleep.

Porn became my way of coping with deeper problems and unmet needs.

Your sexual sin might feel like the biggest problem in your life right now because it is taking up so much space in your mind or because it's controlling your life. While sexual sin is a problem in your life, it's not the *biggest* problem.

For you to be set free, it is critical for you to identify and address the problem beneath your sexual sins. I'll put it bluntly. In some ways, porn worked for me. It distracted me from my loneliness and temporarily numbed my pain. But the "cure" of porn just added to my underlying shame. In order to walk away from my porn use, I had to learn to address the problems porn was hiding.

In what ways do you think porn may be "working for you" as a way to cope with difficulty in your life?

While every woman's story is unique, here are a few common reasons why women turn to pornography or casual sex relationships.

YOU NEED RELATIONSHIPS

Sarah had recently become a Christian. Over lunch, she honestly shared with me (Juli) about her battle to stop having casual sex. "There is this guy I met at work. We barely know each other, but I am attracted to him. We started flirting and the next thing I knew, I found myself in bed with him. How do I stop wanting to have sex with random guys like this?"

I asked her, "Did you feel better after you had sex with him?" She honestly answered no.

Then I asked her to reflect on what she got out of the encounter. Was there any moment during which it was satisfying? "I just wanted to be held and touched. It felt great in the moment to connect to someone even so briefly. And then I felt disgusting and rejected afterward."

We live in a world where it's easy to feel isolated. You weren't created to live in a small apartment all by yourself, working sixty hours a week, and being entertained by a screen during your free time. You were made for intimacy. Whether or not you are married or have children, you need touch, you need to share life with people, and you need to be known.

While our pace of life often sabotages intimacy, it offers sex as a cheap replacement. Sarah didn't hook up for sex. She used sex so she could experience a fleeting moment of connection and affirmation.

Clues that your struggle may be fed by loneliness:

- Temptation is greatest when you are or feel alone.
- Even if you are surrounded by people, you feel isolated, unseen, or unloved.

How would you describe your current community?

What role do you think loneliness might play in your sexual struggle?

YOU NEED COMFORT

When you have sex or masturbate to pornography, your body releases "feel good" chemicals like endorphins, oxytocin, and serotonin. God designed this release to reinforce the bonding between a husband and wife. Over time, a married couple learns to seek comfort and pleasure by pursuing and responding to one another.

Many learn to use sex or masturbation as a form of self-medicating. Sexual temptation is less about the desire to have sex and more about escaping feelings of anxiety, restlessness, or depression.

One of the leading movements combating porn is called Fight the New Drug, reminding us that sex can be misused as a drug because it can hijack the natural pleasure centers of the brain. You then become dependent on the drug to navigate the challenges of life or even to relax or fall asleep. This is not how God intends us to use the gift of sex, whether we are married or not.

As I (Joy) shared earlier, I used pornography and masturbation to cope with the pain and shame I felt from being date-raped. I also became dependent on it to fall asleep.

Clues that your need for comfort might be underlying your sexual desire:

- Your sexual temptation is greatest when you experience physical or emotional discomfort.
- You regularly feel anxious or depressed.
- You use sex to reward yourself for working hard.

What role do you think discomfort and pain may play in your porn use?

What are some specific things that cause you to feel anxious, depressed, or emotionally distressed?

YOU NEED TO BE "SPENT"

Research shows that people who engage in demanding exercise routines have lower sex drives.[5] One reason for this correlation is depleted testosterone by too much work and lack of rest. While depleting our testosterone because of overwork is a bad thing, this also shows that God gives us many ways to direct the energy that may be experienced as a sexual drive.

Testosterone is a "green light" hormone in the body that plays a role in risk-taking, competitive behaviors, energy, and concentration. While the amount of testosterone is greater in men than women, both genders experience a higher libido as testosterone increases. Although it's a bit more complicated than this, think of testosterone as a regularly generated fuel that burns up when you "spend" it.

God gave us testosterone and other brain chemicals not only for their role in sex, but also as a natural means of prompting us to influence our world in meaningful ways. Jay Stringer in his groundbreaking book, *Unwanted*, notes that one of the strongest correlations for people battling pornography is boredom and a lack of purpose.[6] When you wake up every day to exciting projects and challenges, you are addressing your emotional and biological need to positively change the world. You may also find that, by the end of the day, you are too "spent" to think about sex.

Clues that boredom might be underlying your sexual desire:

- You experience more sexual temptation when life seems dull.
- You don't feel challenged in your everyday activities (including work, hobbies, or service).
- You often feel restless at night.

What role do you think boredom might be playing in your sexual struggles?

YOU NEED HEALING

Kaley grew up in a home that looked perfect on the outside, but behind closed doors, her father sexually abused her throughout her childhood. While as an adult Kaley hated sex, she also found herself in a cycle of sexually acting out, followed by self-contempt and shame. She felt like her life was spiraling out of control after two abortions, a life-threatening STD, and the loss of her job because of sexual misconduct.

Why would a woman like Kaley continue to put her life at risk and compromise her future because of sex? Wouldn't the abuse she suffered as a child make her want to avoid sex instead of insatiably seek it?

Trauma from our childhood often plays out and seeks expression in our sexual temptations. This is true not just of childhood sexual trauma, but also our early experiences of feeling out of control, abandoned, neglected, or dominated. We may be drawn to sexual experiences, including porn, as an ineffective way to address painful patterns from the past.

Clues that needing healing might be underlying your sexual desire:

- You find yourself drawn into sexual situations or fantasies that also repel you (for example, BDSM, which stands for bondage, dominance, sadism, and masochism).

- You have a love-hate relationship toward sexual outlets.

- You have significant trauma in your past that you haven't worked through with a counselor.

How might wounds from your past possibly impact your current struggle with pornography or other sexual temptation?

Your journey through this book is going to help you become more aware of the desires and wounds that play into your porn struggle. Overcoming temptation is about more than just saying no. As you grow in your relationship with God, you may find that He helps you address sexual temptation by meeting you in the underlying wellspring of those temptations.

Have you ever considered that your porn use may cover up deeper issues? Why or why not?

Of the four needs listed here (relationships, comfort, activity, and healing), which seems to be the one that most aligns with your experience of sexual temptation?

How We Get Hooked

For many women, their struggle with pornography began early on. Twelve years old is the average age of first exposure to porn.[7] (As an average, that means that many girls are first exposed at even younger ages!) More than half of teens weren't looking for it but were sexually awakened by accidently seeing graphic sexual images or experiences.[8] Like my story, it could be a friend or family member who first opened up the internet to share an exciting image with you. While some women were introduced to porn by a significant other to "learn" about sex, others intentionally look at porn because of curiosity or questions about sex. Online porn is often the sex education of today's teen (and child).

HOW PORN DESTROYS YOUR BRAIN

Many helpful books and documentaries explain the neuroscience of the brain during sexual experiences.[9] This is a short summary of how our brains react:

God created us to experience pleasure when engaging in healthy things like eating good food, going on a walk in nature, or getting a hug. We experience this feeling of pleasure when our brain releases a neurochemical called dopamine. The brain associates the feeling of pleasure with certain activities. When a woman starts by looking at simple images, viewing sexually explicit social media, or reading a romance novel, dopamine gets released, making a connection in the brain that links the action with pleasure. This makes you want to return again and again to that activity. Pornography hijacks this "pleasure center" of your brain so that even normal sexual experiences are no longer exciting or pleasurable.

Looking at the same explicit picture of the same sexting exchange won't give you the same amount of pleasure. This is called "tolerance." You need something different, usually more explicit, to get the same level of pleasure you once experienced.

The more you turn to porn, the more you are reinforcing the addictive behavior, and the more dopamine is needed.[10] The dopamine rush from sexual thoughts or activity is so powerful that it can override your brain's ability to make wise decisions.[11]

Just as with drug addiction, a person can develop a tolerance for and become desensitized to different types of sexual sin. This is often the case for women who start with soft-core porn like erotica. Soon, a woman may turn to hard-core porn. Over time, porn may no longer satisfy her inner desires. Just like in drug addiction, the addict will turn to bigger and harder products.[12] She will need to spend more time viewing porn and changing the variety of images and videos she watches. This was true for me (Joy). I found myself watching things I would never have imagined watching just months before.

Eventually, you might even want to experience what you see in person by acting out sex scenes in relationships.

Not only is sexual sin addictive, but it's damaging to your brain.[13] It reconstructs your neurological pathways and bonds you to the images because God created you for intimacy.

Have you experienced needing more and more sexual encounters and a variety of types to increase your dopamine levels? If so, how does it feel to learn about the addictiveness of a dopamine rush through sexual experiences and how it impacts your brain?

We want to tell you the effects of sexual sin on our brains to point you toward a bigger picture of God's design for sexuality. God created us as sexual beings, and our sexual desires are a good gift from Him! We need to learn how to steward this gift in singleness and marriage. Using porn or casual hookups is a misuse of the powerful experience of sex and will likely cause more pain and loneliness in your life.

WHAT IS SEXUAL ADDICTION?

Not everyone who struggles with sexual sin is addicted. All sexual sin is wrong, but addiction describes a cycle of temptation and sin that feels beyond their power to break.

If you've tried changing your habits and finding healing, but you always end up doing the same thing over and over, then you might be stuck in the cycle of addiction. If you discover that you are addicted to sex or porn, you will need more support than this book can provide. Use this resource as a first step in your process of healing, and find a licensed professional counselor or ministry that has expertise in addressing sexual addiction.

How often is your mind consumed by the thought to turn toward sexual sin? What percentage of your life is filled with unwanted sexual behavior?

Scripture warns us to "not be mastered by anything" (1 Cor. 6:12). Read this verse in context in the passage 1 Corinthians 6:9–20. As a Christian, what does it mean to not be mastered by anything?

FORGING A NEW PATH

The good news is this: we worship a God who redeems and restores our broken sexuality. We believe you will find hope through this book as God reveals your pain and begins to change it "to bestow on [you] a crown of beauty instead of ashes, the oil of joy instead of mourning, and a garment of praise instead of a spirit of despair" (Isa. 61:3).

Not only does God restore the beauty from ashes, but He also restores and renews our brains. We can have hope that even if we have been negatively affected by porn, we can be healed!

God created our brains to constantly be responding to what's going on around us. We can slowly rewire our brains to respond to healthy inputs rather than being flooded by triggers and temptation. This is not a "quick fix" but comes with the determination to honor God with our minds and actions.

Read Ephesians 4:17–24 and focus on verse 23, "to be made new in the attitude of your minds." Another version says, "to be renewed in the spirit of your minds" (Eph. 4:23 ESV). What does it mean to be made new or renewed in our minds?

Write your response to the hope that you can find in knowing God can renew your mind after struggling with the addictiveness of sexual sin.

We are going to spend the rest of this book in the pursuit of freedom. Whether you are addicted to porn or not, God *can* renew your mind, take away your shame, and speak His love into the deepest places in your heart. How do I know? Because He has done it for me! My friend, true freedom is possible, but it's a marathon rather than a sprint. Hang in there because you are not running alone!

The Link Between Porn and Intimacy

Sometimes when we hear "sexual sin is bad," we translate that into "my sexuality is bad." God created us as sexual beings. The act of sexual intimacy is a good gift, created to be a celebration within the covenant of marriage. Your sexual desires are not bad, although they may have been misdirected and twisted by sin. God created you as a woman with longings, hormones, and desires. Having questions and desires about sex is not weird.

Understanding sexual temptation begins with understanding why God created sex in the first place. We will spend an entire week looking at God's purpose for sex in Week 4. But for now, it's important for you to understand that sexual desire is ultimately rooted in a desire for intimacy.

Over the past decade I (Juli) have interacted with thousands of Christians who struggle with a variety of sexual struggles. I've come to this conclusion: We all carry some level of sexual and relational brokenness. You are going through this book because you want to be free of porn or erotica. You have a friend who doesn't struggle with porn, but she spends hours a day on social media. What she sees on the screen has shaped what she buys and how she interacts with people. You and your friend's struggle may be different, but it's also the same.

You don't have a porn problem; you have an intimacy problem.

At its most basic level, you don't have a porn problem; you have an intimacy problem.

Marnie Ferree, a licensed marriage and family therapist who specializes in sexual addiction, writes,

It's not about sex at all, but about the desperate search for love and touch and affirmation and acceptance. Those are descriptions of intimacy. God created us for intimate connection with him, with others and with ourselves. When those connections are broken or absent . . . women desperately seek a false substitute. Sex or an intense relationship [or porn] offers the best stand-in for the real thing.[14]

While we live in a world that encourages sexual exploration, our culture often sabotages intimacy. We are busy, distracted, and simply move on when relationships become difficult. Social media encourages us to present only the best version of ourselves, making us feel like no one could really love us exactly as we are. Feeling isolated and unlovable, we fall for what can feel like a valid substitution.

SEX IS OFTEN A SEARCH FOR INTIMACY

In the beginning of my sexual journey, I (Joy) never actually wanted sex. I wanted to feel loved, cherished, and beautiful. I longed for intimacy. For a split second, I would feel loved, but the moment would fade as my boyfriend put on his clothes and walked out the door. My early sexual curiosities and experiences awakened love at a young age, making it even harder to walk away from sexual activity.

My friend Autumn grew up emotionally and verbally bullied by boys. When she got older, she sought their attention and approval. At age fourteen, Autumn texted her first nude photo. The praise and attention she received felt amazing and she was hooked, even though she knew deep down that it wasn't real love.

"Autumn, if you felt so empty, what made you continue?" I asked.

"I wanted to feel desirable and loved."

Autumn wanted to know if what she was experiencing in real life was "real sex." Her curiosity led her to porn (which turned out to be a bad teacher). At eighteen years old, Autumn continued to lust, send sexually explicit photos of herself to men, and act out what she saw on the screen with her boyfriend, who eventually broke up with her. Autumn shared that the pain and rejection drove her to seek comfort from more than just porn. The porn wasn't enough anymore, and Autumn developed a sex addiction. She spent over a year hooking up with strangers. She felt a thrill of each new partner and then the immediate wave of depression and shame.

Most women don't look at porn for porn's sake. We use pornography because it promises to dull the pain of the past and to make us feel wanted and loved, even for a moment.

Our desire to be loved and find love is not a bad thing. God created marriage, romantic love, and sexual desire. Desiring love is part of our God-given design, but first and foremost God designed us to long for His love.

Have you ever turned to sexual activity to meet an emotional need? If so, how did you feel afterward?

In what ways have you personally experienced our culture offering sexual experience as a replacement for intimacy?

What do you think about your sexual sin issues being intimacy issues? Do you feel like you're lacking intimacy with God and others?

How do your sexual choices reveal your desire to be fully known and fully loved?

A WOMAN WHO LONGED FOR LOVE AND ACCEPTANCE

The book of John includes a story of a woman who felt unloved and searched for acceptance and satisfaction in her life. In fact, she may have had a lot in common with a woman today who struggles with porn. Take a few moments to read her story in John 4.

Here is what we know about her:

- She was a Samaritan. Samaritans were regarded by most Jewish people as not being true seekers of God. Samaritans and Jews carried racial prejudice against each other.

- She had five previous husbands. In the ancient Near East culture, women didn't have the choice to divorce, so this woman likely had been rejected or abandoned by a series of men.

- She was currently living with a man she wasn't married to. Again, we don't know the circumstances that led her to this relationship, but she could have been judged as an immoral woman by her culture.[15]

- She was at the well during the hottest part of the day. It is highly probable that because of her shame, she avoided going to the well when other women would be there.

Here is what we know about how Jesus interacted with this woman:

- He intentionally lingered by this well while His disciples went off to find something to eat.

- By talking to her, Jesus broke cultural and racial barriers, showing her dignity and attention. This woman mattered to Jesus. Jews did everything they could to avoid interacting with Samaritans, including taking the long way around town — but Jesus decided to go right through Samaria.[16]

- He intentionally stepped into the most vulnerable aspect of her life. She didn't volunteer the information about her past and current relationships. Jesus spoke this truth about her.

- He didn't pile on shame, but offered her the greatest hope. He revealed to this woman that He was the Messiah.

- He spoke her language by offering her "living water." Yes, she was physically thirsty, but she had also been relationally thirsty. The water Jesus offered was not physical water, but the water of life-giving love and acceptance. Jesus gave her the opportunity for a relationship with Him and eternal life!

Here was a woman, lonely, isolated, and likely suffocating with sexual shame. Yet when she met Jesus, He knew her fully and loved her completely. Even though she was a Samaritan and He was a Jew, He looked her in the eyes and showed her compassion.

Picture yourself in her shoes, probably lonely or feeling unloved. She likely had trauma in her past from being abused, divorced, widowed, or abandoned. We don't know her story, but Jesus did. We do know that she longed for more, for the living water Jesus offered.

What would change in your life if you lived fully satisfied by the Living Water?

How would believing that Jesus can fully satisfy you guide your struggle against sexual sin?

Friend, Jesus is also the one that you've been waiting for in your search for meaning and fulfillment. Imagine what your life would be like if you actually believed that Jesus' love could satisfy you. What if you woke up each morning knowing that no matter what you did today, how you performed, or how you felt, Jesus would still love you? His love doesn't change. He is constant and always pursuing you.

As we close out this week, you might doubt if Jesus can provide you with eternal water. You may wonder whether the love of God can actually help you experience freedom. The idea that "Jesus loves you" might sound like a nice thought with little real-life promise of making a difference in your current struggles, shame, and pain. If you've had that thought, you are not alone. That's why next week will be all about how you can experience the reality of God's love in your journey toward freedom!

WEEK 1: SMALL GROUP DISCUSSION QUESTIONS

1. Joy shared that she can tell her story because "someone else went first." Talk about your experience of feeling alone in your sexual struggles.

2. How does it feel to know that you are not alone in your struggle with sexual sin?

3. How is pornography, or other sexual sin, affecting your relationship with God right now? How is pornography affecting your relationships with others: friends, family, coworkers, significant others, etc.?

4. How does pornography, or other sexual sin, help you deal with the hard things in your current life or in your past?

5. In Day 2, we looked at reasons why porn isn't your biggest problem. Which of the following reasons did you most relate to? You need relationships. You need comfort. You need to be "spent." You need healing.

6. What do you think about your sexual sin issues being intimacy issues? Do you feel like you're lacking intimacy with God and others?

7. What do you think are some of the deeper heart issues of women who struggle with pornography, erotica, or sexual sin?

8. What are some of your hopes and fears as you begin the freedom journey within this group?

Can God's Love Really Be Enough?

Have you ever sought out intimacy, yet remained unsatisfied? Have you had one of those nights where you feel so unloved or alone? When you wish you could have someone to hold you and tell you he loves you? We need healthy relationships, but the love we experience on earth will never compare to God's love for us. Our hearts have been made to cry out for a love that can only come from our Creator. A man may seem like the best fix, and porn might feel like an okay substitute, but only God's love is a lasting solution.

As a new Christian, I (Joy) remember people saying that my need for intimacy could be met in my relationship with God. Honestly, I didn't understand that. How could God make me feel loved, valued, and cared for when He felt a million miles away? Maybe you've heard people say that God can satisfy your deepest longing and you wonder how that is practically possible. That's where we are headed in our time together this week.

There is not a human being on earth (even those surrounded by good friends and a loving husband) who doesn't know the ache of feeling rejected, unloved, or invisible. Why? Because we were made for intimate fellowship with a God who can seem distant, condemning, or indifferent. Christianity is not a religion of going to church and following rules. It is an invitation to this kind of intimate relationship with the God of the universe. Over the next few days, we will discover three unique aspects of God's invitation to be intimate with you (Father, Savior, and Friend).

The Intimate Love of a Father

Your father, whether or not he was involved in your life, has had a huge impact on you. In many ways, he represents to you your worth and even your relationship with God. No father is perfect. Unfortunately, even well-meaning fathers say and do things that leave wounds—wounds we later try to heal in our dating and sexual relationships.

In today's world, the phrase "daddy issues" is so common that the hashtag #daddyissues often trends on social media. While it is a sarcastic insult on social media, "daddy issues" are no joke. The reality is that the way you see yourself was possibly shaped early in your life by the words and actions of your father.

What is your relationship like with your dad?

In what ways did he represent God's love well for you?

In what ways did he represent God's love poorly for you?

WHAT A GOOD FATHER DOES

God created unique earthly relationships to give us relational road maps for understanding our relationship with Him. One of those relationships is father/daughter. Even if you don't have a good father, you intuitively know what a good father should be and do. In your heart, your ache for a father who never fails and points you to God. Even if your earthly dad fails, your heavenly Father will never fail. The good Father will: protect, provide, discipline, and affirm.

A GOOD FATHER PROTECTS

While our human dads are limited in how they protect us, our heavenly Father isn't. But you may wonder why God has allowed difficult or painful things to happen to you. People in the Bible, such as Job, Rahab, and David, asked that question too. While we don't understand God's ways, you can have confidence in this: God, your Father, never leaves you. He is always with you. His heart is for you. He is a protector.

Read Psalm 18:1–3. In what ways do you long for a Father who will protect you?

What words and phrases from the verses above speak of God as your Father and protector?

A GOOD FATHER PROVIDES

When Jesus taught about our heavenly Father, He made a direct connection to earthly fathers. During one teaching, He said, "Which of you, if your son asks for bread, will give him a stone? Or if he asks for a fish, will give him a snake? If you, then, though you are evil, know how to give good gifts to your children, how much more will your Father in heaven give good gifts to those who ask him!" (Matt. 7:9–11).

Fathers provide good things for their children. When you are lonely and hurting, you might have trouble remembering the good things God has provided for you. Sometimes we can only see what we *lack* instead of remembering what we have.

This is often the case in the areas of singleness and sexuality. If you are unmarried, you may focus on your lack of a spouse instead of God's love for you and the community of friends God has given you. Or you might believe that having a spouse would fix all your problems with sexual sin.

Take a moment to read Psalm 104. Make a list of all the ways God provides as reflected in this psalm.

Can you think of any "lacks" that you tend to focus on more than the gifts God has already provided?

What are three specific ways God is providing for you right now?

A GOOD FATHER DISCIPLINES

One of the ways God shows His fatherly love for you is through His discipline. Love sets boundaries. Discipline is often seen as a negative word, but discipline is how parents protect their children from touching hot stoves or running into the street. Discipline saves lives!

What if you could look at porn ten hours a day and never feel miserable? Do you really want God to take away your feelings of sadness and guilt when you are in the middle of sin? If you no longer feel sadness or guilt when watching porn, your heart may have hardened. Your first step might be praying to God and asking Him to show you the darkness of your sin. That is God's discipline, calling you to repentance and freedom. God doesn't discipline you because He is mad at you, but because He loves you.

Hebrews 12 reminds us:

> "My [daughter], do not make light of the Lord's discipline,
>   and do not lose heart when he rebukes you,
> because the Lord disciplines the one he loves,
>   and he chastens everyone he accepts as his [child]." (Heb. 12:5-7)

How are you experiencing God's discipline in this season of your life?

How is that discipline an expression of your Father's love?

A GOOD FATHER AFFIRMS

From the time you were born you have longed for your daddy's love, approval, and affection. There is a good chance that nothing mattered more than your father's opinion of you. If your dad was absent or unloving, you doubted and questioned a lot of things: "What is wrong with me?" "If my earthly father doesn't love me, how will God?" "If my earthly dad doesn't think I'm beautiful, how will a man?"

While many of us never got that approval from our earthly fathers, God loves us with unconditional adoration! You are His precious daughter. When I (Juli) struggled with the love of my earthly father, the Lord spoke very tenderly to me from these verses in the Psalms:

Though my father and mother forsake me, the LORD will receive me! (Ps. 27:10)

Listen, daughter, and pay careful attention: Forget your people and your father's house. Let the king be enthralled by your beauty; honor him, for he is your lord. (Ps. 45:10–11)

Whatever words your dad has said to you, whatever actions you've done or have had done to you, know that you are never beyond repair of the redeeming love and power of God your heavenly Father. The truth about God your Father can get lost if you only see God through the lens of your earthly dad. When you realize your daddy issues, you may realize your God issues.

When you realize your daddy issues, you may realize your God issues.

Our view and relationship with our earthly dad is reflected in our view and relationship with our heavenly Dad. For this reason, it is incredibly important to find the truth in Scripture and read how God views you, His precious daughter.

How God Views You

- Your heavenly Dad proclaims that you are "fearfully and wonderfully made" (Ps. 139:14).

- If you doubt your earthly dad's love for you, know that your heavenly Father says you are "more precious than rubies" (Prov. 3:15).

- If your earthly dad says or thinks you aren't good enough, remember that your heavenly Dad called "you out of darkness into his wonderful light," and "you are a chosen people, a royal priesthood, a holy nation, God's special possession" (1 Peter 2:9).

- If your earthly father is hateful, know that your heavenly Dad is like a father to His children; tender and "compassionate on those who fear him" (Ps. 103:13).

- If your earthly father takes out his anger on you, believe that your heavenly Dad is righteous and seeks "justice for all the oppressed" (Ps. 103:6).

- If your dad refuses to forget your past mistakes, remember that the Lord doesn't hold your past mistakes against you: "as far as the east is from the west, so far has he removed our transgressions from us" (Ps. 103:12).

- If your earthly dad leaves your family or chooses another family, know that your heavenly Father always "goes with you; he will never leave you nor forsake you" (Deut. 31:6).

- If your earthly father is physically or emotionally abusive, believe that "the righteous person may have many troubles, but the LORD delivers [you] from them all" (Ps. 34:19).

- If your earthly dad fails to live up to his fatherly responsibilities and fails to provide for you, "do not be afraid, little flock, for your Father has been pleased to give you the kingdom" (Luke 12:32).

No earthly father is perfect. The good news is that our heavenly Father is perfect. Our heavenly Father can and will be there in every way our earthly father can't.

No matter what your relationship with your dad looks like, know that your identity is not found in your earthly father's love. Your identity is found in our heavenly Father's love. A dad's love will not fill the empty space in your heart, and neither will that of a husband. Only the infinite love of our Father will fulfill our desire to feel fully known and fully loved. Once we begin to understand that we need only the Father's love, we can begin to find freedom from sexual shame and addiction.

Looking back at your childhood, can you identify wounds that still need healing?

What is one practical step you can take today to start believing you are God's precious, beloved, and beautiful daughter?

Do you fully believe that God's fatherly love is enough, even if your earthly dad's love is missing?

The Intimate Love of a Savior

If, like me (Joy), you've longed to be loved by a man, you're not alone. The Bible tells stories of women who have felt the same way. The heartbreaking story of Leah is found in the book of Genesis. Over and over again, Leah attempted to win the love of her husband, Jacob, but he loved her younger sister, Rachel, his second wife. Leah's name, which means "weary," seems to appropriately describe how she felt much of her life.

The Bible describes the sisters this way: "Leah had weak eyes, but Rachel had a lovely figure and was beautiful" (Gen. 29:17). If you have a sister, perhaps you can relate to this story. Maybe you were the less popular sister. Maybe teachers compared your grades. Maybe boys made comments about your appearances as sisters. It can hurt to be compared to our siblings.

Jacob had worked for the sisters' father, Laban, for seven years to be allowed to marry Rachel, his first choice. But Laban tricked Jacob into marrying Leah instead. (Yes, Leah had some serious "daddy issues" too!) Jacob and Leah were married, but Jacob publicly professed his love for Rachel. (Imagine trying to earn someone's love for years only to be met with rejection after rejection.) After agreeing to serve Laban for an additional seven years, Jacob was allowed to also marry Rachel. The Bible says that, "Jacob made love to Rachel also, and his love for Rachel was greater than his love for Leah" (29:30). Ouch.

After all this, when God "saw that Leah was not loved, he enabled her to conceive" (29:31). God saw Leah and provided for her. God gave her a baby. Leah gave birth and said, "Surely my husband will love me now" (29:32). Nope. Jacob still loved Rachel more. So she conceived two more times, hoping that finally Jacob would love her. Leah said, "Now at last my husband will become attached to me, because I have borne him three sons" (29:34). Nope. Imagine the physical pain of carrying and giving birth to three babies and the emotional pain of your husband not loving you. Leah just kept hoping.

Finally, Leah realized that God alone could fill this void. She conceived another child and said, "This time I will praise the LORD" (29:35). While Leah may never have experienced the love of Jacob, God graced Leah and showed her His love in a special way. Leah named her son Judah, and it was through his lineage that Jesus, the Savior, would enter the world.

After reading Leah's story, could you relate with her? Have you ever been picked second? Have you tried to get someone to love you, only to be rejected again and again? If so, share about that time.

Like Leah, I longed to be loved. From countless failed attempts to find love and approval from my dad, boys, and friends, I finally found the love I sought years later—at the feet of my Savior. As a college freshman, I desired the love of Christ above all else and surrendered my promiscuous lifestyle.

Perhaps you've never truly felt genuine love from a man. It's possible that you grew up without the love of a father figure, or you've endured mistreatment from men. As a woman struggling with unwanted sexual sin, you may ask, "Can God truly love and forgive a sinner like me?" There is good news for you. God loves you and longs for a personal relationship with you. His affection for you is so profound that He sent Jesus to sacrifice Himself on the cross for your sins. Nothing you do (or don't do) will cause God to love you any more or less. You are never too far gone or out of His reach! He loves you unconditionally, even in the midst of your struggles.[17]

Why do you think people doubt God's love when struggling with sexual sin and shame?

What makes you doubt God's love for you?

HOW GOD SHOWS YOU HIS LOVE

God sent His only Son, Jesus, as a powerful demonstration of how much He loves you. You may have grown up hearing "Jesus saved you by dying on the cross," but take some time to let the truth of that sink in. Saving someone is a powerful and loving response to helplessness.

Several years ago, I (Juli) had a severe allergic reaction to some medication. I was home alone with two of my boys, who were four and two at the time. As soon as I realized what was happening to me, I called 911, told my four-year-old to watch his little brother, and unlocked the front door, knowing that I might be unconscious by the time the ambulance arrived. Sure enough, I blacked out. When I woke up, paramedics were swarming around me. A neighbor saw the ambulance and came over to take care of my little boys.

Over the next hour, I vomited all over the place. One paramedic cleaned me up while another strapped me to a gurney. I was helpless. In that moment, they were my saviors. They didn't ask for my credit card. They didn't care what I looked like, how good of a person I was, or what I could offer them. They were there to serve and to save my life. Even though I don't know their names, I am deeply grateful for them. In the "saving" process, they touched, assessed, and cleaned my body in ways no stranger would do. Both the act of being saved and my gratitude afterward were uniquely intimate experiences of being cared for.

This saving care is also true of God. He didn't save you because you deserved it or earned it. He saved you because He loves you. He is love. In many ways, the deepest intimacy you can experience with God is to understand the depths of His salvation. Like a paramedic, He doesn't politely stand by while you suffer, but steps into the most intimate places of your life. He gets His hands "dirty" with your shame and your sin. He is mighty to save!

Sometimes we run away from God's love because we don't understand that He is the Savior. A savior doesn't look at things for what's in it for them. They save because that is who they are. God is the perfect Savior! All you have to do is call Him and unlock the door.

Describe a time when you were helpless, in need of someone to save you. What happened?

Being saved requires admitting our inability to help ourselves. How might your independence keep you from experiencing the saving love of God?

How is being saved an intimate experience? How does God's love as your Savior build your intimacy with Him?

The Bible is filled with passages that show us a glimpse into the amazing love of God. Even when we have nothing to offer God, He saved us and loved us completely.

Look up the verses below. As you read through them, think about God's love for you.

- John 15:12–16
- Romans 5:8
- Romans 8:38–39
- 1 John 4:9–10
- Ephesians 2:8–9

What do these verses teach us about God's love?

God's love for us is complex, fascinating, and beautiful. His love for us could only happen through the death of Jesus. It is hard to comprehend that we humans are so sinful that Jesus had to die for us in order for a perfect God to love us. Jesus' death was God's greatest act of love and salvation.

God knows you completely and loves you fully. His love is greater than anything you have done. Reread this: **God knows you completely and loves you fully. God's love is greater than anything you have done.** This line might be very hard for you to believe, but it is the truth!

The Intimate Love of a Friend

Who is your BFF? Who is the first person you want to tell when something good happens and the person you immediately text when your world is caving in?

We all need "that person." Maybe your mom, your husband, your roommate, your sister. Or perhaps you honestly answer "no one."

Can you imagine God being a friend like that? I (Juli) couldn't either until I spent time with my friend Linda. She was in her seventies when I met her, and had spent most of her life on the mission field. As Linda and I began to get to know one another, I noticed that she talked about God as if He were always in the room. I had been a Christian for more than thirty years, but had no idea how I could have an actual friendship with God. My relationship with Linda awakened something inside of me. I longed for an intimacy with God that I honestly didn't think was possible.

Have you ever met someone like Linda who has an intimate friendship with God? If so, describe what you've learned from them.

What do you think it means for God to be your friend?

Do you believe you can have an actual friendship with God? Why or why not?

I know what you might be thinking. That kind of relationship with God is for "super believers" like Moses who get to see God while the rest of us wander around. I thought that too, until I discovered this truth: I have exactly as much of God as I really want. God says, "You will find me when you seek me with your whole heart" (Jer. 29:13). God wants to be sought and He wants to be found.

Read Jeremiah 29:11–14. You might be familiar with verse 11, but focus on the verses that follow. What is stopping you from seeking God with your whole heart?

How would your life be different if you did seek God with your whole heart? How would it impact your freedom journey?

Jesus said to His disciples toward the end of His life, "I no longer call you servants . . . . Instead, I have called you friends" (John 15:15). Jesus' relationship with His disciples serves as an example of the intimacy we can share with God. Yes, God is still our Father and our Savior. He is perfect and holy unlike any other friend you might have. He is worthy of our worship, our adoration, and our praise. Yet, He still extends His friendship!

To make this real for you, let's look at five characteristics of a good friend and how you can know God as that kind of friend.

A FRIEND IS SOMEONE I CAN COUNT ON

A few years ago, I (Juli) went through a very difficult season where I experienced a heavy cloud of shame. As much as I tried, I couldn't seem to shake it. The shame haunted me so deeply that I considered stepping away from ministry. After about three months of trying to deal with the battle largely on my own, I traveled to Colorado where two of my best friends lived. I poured out my heart and my tears to each of them and they comforted me. They cried with me, hugged me, prayed over me, and spoke words of life into my doubts.

These friends are so valuable to me that I flew across the country to see them in my time of need.

God is that kind of friend. He cares about your burdens and your shame. You can be honest with Him about your struggle, and you don't have to fly on an airplane to see Him! The kindest, most compassionate person you know is just an echo of the kind of friend God wants to be to you.

A FRIEND IS SOMEONE WHO CAN RELATE TO ME

Friendships are formed through a common bond. Sometimes God doesn't feel like a friend because He is so different from us. How could the God of the universe understand my loneliness, my weakness, my fear, and my shame?

God went out of His way to be close to us. In the person of Jesus Christ, He experienced everything you could possibly experience on earth. Pain, hunger, rejection, temptation, betrayal. You might think, "Jesus never struggled with porn. He doesn't know what it feels like to be burdened by shame."

While aspects of His life were very different from yours, Jesus experienced every human emotion you have gone through. Even though He didn't sin, He carried *our sins*. He knows the weight of them.

Read Hebrews 4:14–16. How does it feel to know that Jesus empathizes with your weaknesses and was tempted in every way?

A FRIEND IS SOMEONE I DON'T HAVE TO PRETEND WITH

Sometimes we think we have to "clean up" our act to be around God. And so to us, God may feel less like a friend and much more like a drill instructor. I don't know why we have this view of God. David, who had an especially intimate relationship with God, honestly expressed his true feelings. David let it all out, like he would with a good friend.

You may rightfully feel like you have to hide your sin struggle from some people in your life, but don't ever feel like you have to (or even can!) pretend with God.

A FRIEND IS SOMEONE WHO TELLS ME THE TRUTH

"Wounds from a friend can be trusted, but an enemy multiplies kisses" (Prov. 27:6). How could a friend's wounds be a good thing? Because a true friend will tell you the truth in love. She will tell you if you should reconsider your hairstyle, if you have a piece of lettuce in your teeth, and if you are making a terrible decision.

Jesus is a friend who will tell you the truth. You might not like the truth, but only the truth can set you free.

A FRIEND IS SOMEONE WHO I REGULARLY TALK TO

While you may have friends who you don't see all the time, the deepest intimacy is created when you have regular (even daily) contact with someone. They are with you in your ups and downs and help you navigate the daily challenges of life.

This is the kind of friendship Jesus offers you. He used the example of a vine being attached to the branch to describe how close we are to be to Jesus. Inseparable. Prayer is not just something you do during your devotions. It is the ongoing fellowship and communication with God through the Holy Spirit.

Of the characteristics of a good friend listed above, which one do you think is the easiest to experience in your relationship with God?

Which one do you struggle believing is possible in your friendship with God?

To develop a friendship with God, you have to spend time getting to know Him. In tomorrow's lesson, we will share some very specific things you can do to develop this kind of relationship with God: your Father, your Savior, and your Friend!

How God's Love Becomes Personal

As you've read the past three days about intimacy with God, perhaps you've felt like that kind of relationship is out of reach for you. God wants to be found! He offers intimacy to anyone who will say yes to the invitation.

You can spend your whole life going to church and still not know God. He wants a relationship with you that is so intimate that you feel safe telling Him everything. He wants you to spend time learning to trust Him.

I (Joy) used to be afraid to come to God with my porn issue. I thought He wouldn't love me anymore if He knew what I was really thinking about (funny because our God knows everything and already knew my thoughts). I had to change my mindset and learn to come to God during temptation and not wait until after I had sinned. God can handle the thoughts we have when we're being tempted, and He can help us run to freedom instead of back into bondage.

Think about your relationship with God. How intimate is it? Would you run to Him in the midst of temptation? Do you feel safe telling Him how you feel? Can you go to Him with your hardest questions?

If you lack that intimacy with God, know that your relationship will not grow and deepen unless you engage with Him. As we wrap up this week, consider these three important practices that will nurture your relationship with God, your Father, your Savior, and your Friend.

READ THE BIBLE AS GOD'S LOVE LETTER

When I (Joy) began pursuing a deep level of intimacy with Jesus, my whole life changed. The first time I experienced this, I was in the midst of healing from the sexual trauma I experienced in college. I was all alone, in a pit of suffering, and all I had was my Bible to turn to for comfort. In times of anger, pain, and loneliness, the Lord met me and provided peace and joy. He satisfied my desire for love as I read His Word.

Did you know that the Bible is God's love letter to us? God inspired the authors of the Bible so He could reveal to us His heart, His plan, and His character. The Bible can feel like a very complicated book to understand. It is composed of smaller books that contain history, prophecy, poetry, and instructions for living.

It is important to study the Bible and to learn how to understand it within the context in which God inspired it. But the Bible is not only a book to study; we also need to personally interact with it. Juli shared earlier how God used passages in the Psalms to speak to her in a time of difficulty. God has used Isaiah 43 in my life to minister to my insecurity and fear of being unloved. As I studied this chapter, I wrote it out in my own words.

I read this passage as if God had hand-written me a love letter in beautiful calligraphy. I wrote it in my journal in the exact same way:

My daughter Joy,

I created you. I formed you. Fear not, for I have redeemed you. I have called you by name. You are Mine. When you pass through the waters, I'll be with you. The waters won't overwhelm you. When you walk through fire, you won't be burned. And the flame shall not consume you. I am the Lord your God, your Savior. The Holy One. You are precious in My eyes and honored, and I love you. Fear not, for I am with you. I created you for My glory. I formed you and made you. I want you to know and believe Me and understand that I am He. The Lord. There was none before Me and none will come after Me. Don't remember the pains of the past, I am doing new things. I formed you so you would praise Me. You aren't giving Me all your heart, you aren't satisfied in Me, instead you have burdened Me with your sins. But I am your God. I blot out your transgressions for My own sake. I will not remember your sins.

Love, Your heavenly Father

Did you catch that God said *I love you*?! Read the exact verse in Isaiah: "Since you are precious and honored in my sight, and because I love you" (43:4). God loves us and

He has written us love letters. In the New Testament, we learn more about how this love extends to us personally. We learn that God loved us before we loved Him. In fact, even when we were dead in our sins, and could do nothing for God, He extended His love to us (Eph. 2:4-5). God's love is not conditional, but flows from His character. God doesn't say, "I love you only if you do this . . . or act like this . . . or only when you stop looking at porn." God loves us through and through.

Read Paul's words in Ephesians 3:16–19. What do these verses tell you about God's love toward you?

Write these verses in your own words, personalizing the message as it applies to you.

SPEAK GOD'S LOVE LANGUAGE

Gary Chapman's bestselling book *The 5 Love Languages* has transformed countless marriages and friendships. Once you understand someone's "love language," you can be sure to communicate your affection in a way that paves the way for intimacy.

Did you know God has a love language? In fact, He told the Israelites that they were wasting their time in religion because they were not speaking His love language! "I hate, I despise your religious festivals; your assemblies are a stench to me" (Amos 5:21). Why? Because God's love language is an obedient and repentant heart. David understood this: "You do not delight in sacrifice, or I would bring it; you do not take pleasure in burnt offerings. My sacrifice, O God, is a broken spirit; a broken and contrite heart you, God, will not despise" (Ps. 51:16–17).

God wants us to love Him with our obedience. Jesus said this clearly: "If you love me, keep my commands" (John 14:15). You could dance in the aisles of church and sign up for every Bible study and still not be developing intimacy with the Lord. He wants your obedience. Intimacy means giving all of yourself.

Do you have areas of your life that you've reserved for yourself, refusing to obey the Lord? If so, what are they?

This kind of obedience and surrender don't imply perfection. God isn't asking you to promise that you will be perfect in resisting porn or other sexual temptation. He is asking for you to repent and place your trust in Him through the struggle. Don't let there be compartments of your life that are kept from Him. Invite Him into your struggle and pain. God's love language is an authentic heart that is fully surrendered to Him.

LOVE GOD WITH YOUR *HEART*

When I (Juli) began to go deeper into intimacy with the Lord, I remembered the verse, "Love the LORD your God with all your heart and with all your soul and with all your strength" (Deut. 6:5). Although I'd read the verse a thousand times, this particular morning I was stuck on the word *heart*. *Do I really love God with my heart? What does that even look like?*

I know what it is to love Mike, my husband, with my heart. I love my kids that way too. But God? How could I love Him with affection?

The deepest growth in intimacy in my personal walk with God began when I made personal worship a daily priority. Worship is how I express affection to my Savior. It is how I give my admiration and love to my heavenly Father.

As someone who loves to *think*, this was a challenge for me. I'd much rather study the Bible than be affectionate with God! Yet, God wants more than my mind—He wants my heart.

Most days, the first thing I do (after brushing my teeth) is to get on my knees in the early hours of the morning and praise God. Often I put on worship tunes to help me express my affection for God. Sometimes in the privacy of my home, I fall on my face or raise my hands in praise. I want every cell of my body to express and declare that I love God!

What do you think it looks like to love God with "all your heart"?

What are some ways you can express your love for God?

You may have some of your own rhythms that help you nurture intimacy with God. Yours don't have to look like ours, but here is the takeaway: you have an intimacy problem that only God can solve. Yes, work on friendships. Yes, pray for a loving husband. Those are wonderful blessings. But ultimately, only nurturing your relationship with God as your Father, your Savior, and your Friend will satisfy that deepest longing for love!

WEEK 2: SMALL GROUP DISCUSSION QUESTIONS

1. What was your relationship like with your dad? In what ways did he represent God's love well for you? In what ways did he represent God's love poorly for you?

2. Why do you think people doubt that God's love can really be enough when struggling with sexual sin and shame?

3. Do you believe God's love is enough to set you free from sexual sin and shame? Why or why not?

4. Do you believe you can have an actual friendship with God? Why or why not?

5. Share examples of friendships in your life that are good reflections of God as a friend.

6. After reading the story about Leah, could you relate with her? Share a time when you felt rejected or overlooked.

7. Share about a time when you felt too dirty to approach God. What would change in your life if you truly believed all you needed to do was run into His arms right now (as opposed to clean up first and then run to Him)?

8. On Day 4 you read about practical ways to nurture your relationship with God. Which one can you intentionally pursue this week?

A New Vision for Sexual Wholeness

Think for a moment about two words: sexual wholeness. What do you imagine it means to be sexually whole?

You probably know what it feels like to be sexually broken. You know the experience of shame that covers you after yet another failure to resist temptation. You may be familiar with rejection and feeling not quite good enough. All around you are other women who seem to be sexually whole—pure, satisfied, beautiful, desired—but that feels like a reality far, far away.

Depending on your age and background, you might be familiar with something called "purity culture." This term describes a movement in the 1990s and early 2000s within Christian settings that encouraged young women and men to "save sex for marriage." Whether or not you grew up hearing purity culture messages, the mantra to remain a virgin until marriage has likely been part of your understanding of what it means to be sexually whole from God's perspective.

The Bible without question tells us that God created sexual expression to be within marriage (we will talk more about that later this week). Having sex outside of marriage is sinful. Pornography is sinful. That is why repentance and grace are key aspects of your freedom journey.

However, when we only think of sexual wholeness by a standard of "purity," we miss the larger message of the Bible. Your purity does not come through saving sex for marriage. Your purity is only through trusting in the righteousness of Jesus Christ!

Over the past several years, I (Juli) have come to love the term "sexual integrity." We sometimes think of purity as a pass-fail test. Either you are a virgin or you aren't. Either you have kept yourself sexually pure or you haven't. By that standard, we have all at some level failed. After all, Jesus said if you are not sexually pure in your thoughts, you are not sexually pure (see Matt. 5:28).

Sexual integrity, however, means that we strive to live in a way that reflects the wholeness and purity that *we have* as daughters of God. It's not something we are trying to earn, but a truth that we are learning to walk out.

Our English word "integrity" comes from the root Latin word "integer," which means to be whole or undivided.

Our friend Julia defined sexual integrity this way:

The first thing that comes to my mind is pizza! A whole pizza is made up of parts, and when each part is present, we call that a whole pizza (this is making me hungry). Or what about a family reunion? You might say, "This year the *whole family* is going to be there," indicating that all will be there in person and accounted for, none missing or absent. It helps me to think of sexual wholeness in this context. That first and foremost, it is a posture before God, where I present all of the pieces of my heart before Him, with none missing or left out. All areas of my heart including—and perhaps especially—the broken ones are exposed, the mask taken off, and brought into the light.

The opposite of integrity is to be "disintegrated" or living a life that has compartments. Have you ever felt like that? With one part of your life, you love and worship God. With another part, you gossip, hate people, or look at porn. "Disintegrity" is not just when we choose to sin, but also when we don't integrate the *whole* truth of God into our lives. You can also lack integrity as a Christian by being stuck in shame, refusing to believe that Jesus can forgive you and set you free.

"Dis-integrity" is not just when we choose to sin, but also when we don't integrate the whole truth of God into our lives.

The truth is, we are all on a journey toward integrity. Your journey toward sexual wholeness is not about sinless perfection. Instead, it is the journey toward the complete surrender of your sexuality for the glory of God.

This week, you will discover a new understanding of sexual wholeness. You don't need a purity pledge and you don't need a spotless history. You can only be pure because of what Christ has *already done* for you on the cross.

Embracing the Right "Story" of Sex

When we were about three years old, we each started asking a question we've been asking our entire lives. *Why?* Deep within us is a curiosity to understand the why behind everything. When we were little, we wanted to know why some people didn't have hair on their heads or why we had to eat spinach or why we had to take a nap. As we grew older, our whys became more complicated. Why do some people suffer more than others? Why isn't our life working out the way we think it should?

Over the past decade, as I (Juli) have been knee-deep in a ministry around sexuality, I've seen that we have a lot of *whys* related to God and sex:

Why is it wrong to have sex outside of marriage?
Why would God give me sexual desires and no outlet for them?
Why won't God take away my sinful desires?

Unfortunately, most of these whys go unanswered. We learn to tuck away our whys, even as they subconsciously torment us.

Christian resources on sex often talk a lot about the *how* you should live, and this is very important. But understanding the *why* gives us context and courage to walk out the *how*. Instead of burying your whys about sex, God wants us to bring them to Him.

What why questions do you have about God and sex?

How have your why *questions been ignored rather than explored or encouraged?*

Do you believe God wants us to ask why?

UNDERSTANDING THE WHY

All of your *why* questions about sex boil down to one big question: What is the purpose of our sexuality?

As you have tried to make sense of your sexuality, you may not realize how much you have been influenced by how our culture answers this question. We live in a world that has framed a very clear answer for the *why* of sex. Throughout your lifetime, you have been inundated with messages that reinforce this belief: sexual exploration and satisfaction are key parts of living a happy life.

Without God as a reference point, we are left to discover our own purposes for sexuality. Sex becomes about satisfaction, identity, and discovery. Just notice this theme in almost every show or movie: a young girl is growing up or going to college and believes that she has to discover herself through sexual experimentation—hookups, trying on new sexual identities, or having sex in a serious romantic relationship. The message is clear. To find out who you are, you have to discover your sexual self.

Growing up, this is what I (Joy) was taught to believe about sex. I had friends who told me I had to try different things and explore my sexuality as an unmarried woman so I knew what I would like once I entered a dating relationship. This is a similar lie we are told about porn, too—that we have to watch porn to explore our sexuality and see what we like.

Sexual wholeness begins with realizing that this is the wrong answer to our *why* questions.

GOD'S STORY OF *WHY*

Through the pages of the Bible, we discover that God provides a very different purpose for our sexuality. *God created our sexuality as a way to reveal how He loves us.*

Everything God created in the physical world reveals something to us about God. Just think of plants, stars, mountains, and animals. The Bible refers to these physical things to teach us about spiritual truths. The same is true of common human experiences. Over and over again, Jesus referred to hunger and thirst, bread and water, to explain who He is and why He came. If you have never experienced physical thirst, you wouldn't understand what Jesus meant when He said, referring to Himself, "whoever drinks the water I give them will never thirst" (John 4:14). If babies were not born, we would have no understanding of when Jesus told Nicodemus, "Very truly I tell you, no one can see the kingdom of God unless they are born again" (John 3:3).

God created our physical bodies to contain echoes of what our souls were created for. This is true of your sexuality. You were not created for sex, but for intimacy. Everything about your physical sexuality helps you understand the intimacy that God created you for.

Read Psalm 19:1–6 and Romans 1:20. What do these passages say about how God reveals Himself through creation?

What is your response to the concept that God reveals Himself through our human experiences?

The Bible is filled with references to this. Ephesians 5:22–33 is a teaching on marriage. Paul repeats what Moses wrote in Genesis, "That is why a man leaves his father and mother and is united to his wife, and they become one flesh" (Gen. 2:24). Then Paul comments, "This is a profound mystery—but I am talking about Christ and the church" (Eph. 5:32).

Read Ephesians 5:22–31. List ways that Paul says the emotional, spiritual, and physical oneness of marriage helps us understand how Christ Jesus loves the church.

Friend, your sexual urges are physical reminders that you were made for intimacy—not primarily with a man, but with the God who created you.

Sex is so powerful, so spiritual, and so important because of what it was created to teach us. God pursues us with a passionate, faithful, and intimate love. We were created for a "marriage" covenant with Him. This is why in the Old Testament, God compared the Israelites to an unfaithful wife when they worshiped other gods. The physical experience of sex and marriage point to the spiritual experience of our relationship with God.

This is why God gave us rules about how we steward our sexuality. Marriage, sexuality, and gender all matter to God because of what they were created to teach us.

What is your response to the idea that sexuality reveals to us God's love?

Do you believe God cares about your sexuality? Why or why not?

How does this challenge your understanding of why God cares about your sex life?

If your sexuality is all about finding a fulfilled and happy life, saying no to temptation will be very difficult. You might even think God is cruel for withholding pleasure from you. But if you understand that God ultimately wants to teach you about true, covenant love through your sexual journey, you will begin to realize that fulfillment is found by following God. Sexual integrity isn't ultimately about what we say no to, but the God we say yes to. This is true for your journey with pornography.

I want to share a quote that I first heard from a pastor that perfectly sums up my experience, "Freedom is not the absence of something, it is the presence of someone."[1]

That someone is Jesus. We spend so much time focusing on our sin that we sometimes forget to focus on the One who died for our sin. We have to remember the fact that we can't earn freedom. We can't expect to walk in freedom by trying harder. We walk in freedom when we walk with God.

> *Sexual integrity isn't ultimately about what we say no to, but the God we say yes to.*

Why Gender Matters

While this book is specifically focused on pornography, you may also have questions about the integrity of same-sex sexual relationships and gender identity. You might have been introduced to these themes *through* pornography. While we will not focus on sexual orientation and gender identity in this book, God's design for sexuality includes embracing the importance of male and female. God's story of sex is a *gendered* story. Yes, male and female can be complicated in today's culture. So can our attractions! However, God has consistently communicated to us through His Word that we cannot embrace the right story of sex while de-emphasizing that He has created us male and female. As followers of God, having integrity means we strive to bring all of our desires, relationships, and wounds before the Lord.

What Does Sexual Wholeness Look Like?

The next two days, we are going to get practical about wholeness. While it is really important for you to understand why God created you as a sexual person, remember: the *why* is meant to translate into a very real *how* we steward the gift of sexuality.

In many ways, living with sexual integrity is even more comprehensive than trying to live with sexual purity. God doesn't just want your behavior to change, He wants to radically impact your thinking, your affections, and your identity.

How would you describe the difference between seeking sexual purity and sexual integrity?

Paul, the same man who wrote about sexuality and marriage pointing to Christ and His bride in Ephesians, also gave us some practical advice on how we live out this why in daily life. Today, we are going to look at his instruction in a letter found in 1 Corinthians.

Even though Paul wrote this letter two thousand years ago, the people he wrote to were not that different from you and me. Sure, they didn't have mobile devices or the internet to tempt them, but sexual sin was a major part of ancient Roman culture. Paul was writing to new Christians who were confused about what it looked like to walk out their faith in their sexuality.

SEXUAL WHOLENESS AND IDENTITY

Identity is the first and foremost foundational step in sexual wholeness. Why? Because you will live out what you believe to be true about you.

Read 1 Corinthians 6:9–11.

Paul is getting ready to teach about sexual wholeness, but his statement about identity is foundational. It is very possible (even likely) that some of the Christians who read this letter still struggled with sins like slander, lust, and greed. Yet their struggles and sins no longer defined who they were. Some people believe that their identity can only change once they clean up their behavior. The opposite is true. God gives us the power to change what we *do* by first redefining who we *are*.

Why is this passage about your identity an important foundation for sexual wholeness?

What is the significance of Paul writing "that is what some of you were" (1 Cor. 6:11)?

In another letter to the same people, Paul wrote, "Therefore, if anyone is in Christ, the new creation has come: The old has gone, the new is here!" (2 Cor. 5:17). How has God given you a new identity, even if you continue to struggle with temptation?

Do you believe that "you were washed, you were sanctified, you were justified in the name of the Lord Jesus Christ and by the Spirit of our God" (1 Cor. 6:11)? Why or why not?

How are you allowing your past sexual sin or current struggle to continue to define you?

While God cares deeply about your sexual behavior, your journey toward sexual wholeness must begin with a radical shift in how you see yourself in Christ Jesus. You are not your sin! You are not your temptation! You are not your shame! When you truly begin to embrace your new identity, your thoughts and desires will begin to change. The journey of growing in your relationship with God is the journey of growing in your faith to *believe* what He says about you. This is why just trying to stop looking at porn will not work in the long run if you are not also doing the work of exposing the lies you believe. (We will tackle this move in Week 5.)

SEXUAL WHOLENESS AND IMMORALITY

As you continue reading in 1 Corinthians 6, you will see Paul dive right into how we, with our new identity as God's people, should view sexual sin.

Read verses 12–20.

Here are some key points Paul makes in this passage about sexual wholeness:

- If you belong to Christ, you no longer have the right to decide for yourself what you will do sexually. The Spirit of God lives in you! So, your goal is to honor Him with your body.

- Your sexual choices matter. Having sex is not the same thing as choosing to eat a cheeseburger. There is something sacred about your sexuality.

- God wants you to run away from any form of sexual immorality. This would include sexual fantasy or activity outside of a marriage covenant between a man and a woman.

- Where we read the phrase "sexual immorality," Paul used the Greek word *porneia*. You can probably figure out that this is the root of the word "pornography." *Porneia* is a broad term used to describe anything that distorts God's design for sexuality. Remember, God's design for sex is to point to covenant love. When sexual expression happens outside of a man and a woman in covenant (marriage), that is sexual immorality (or sexual sin).

- Sexual sin is different from any other sin. Some people translate this as "sexual sin is unforgivable or worse than any other sin." This conclusion is not consistent with Scripture. However, it does show us that God created sex to communicate something unique through our bodies. Sex is never just sex. It has a spiritual component to it woven within the fabric of our biology. This is why you are likely to remember a hookup from five years ago when you can't remember that you lied or gossiped. Both are sin and serious before the Lord. We also see the very practical application of this in the fact that sex can lead to physical consequences like pregnancy, STDs, and changes in how our brains are wired.

Is masturbation a form of sexual sin?

This question is a bit complicated because the Bible never mentions masturbation. When the Bible doesn't address something directly, we lean on principles we can apply that God has been clear about. Here are three specific principles to consider:

1. It's the thought that counts.

While masturbation may not be specifically named a sin, the sexual fantasies that usually go with it are sinful. As Jesus stated, this is adultery of the heart (Matt. 5:28). Any time you are viewing, reading about, or thinking about something sexual for the purpose of arousal (apart from a married couple thinking sexually about each other), you are promoting lustful thoughts.

2. Remember the purpose of sexuality.

One of the greatest dangers of masturbation is the belief that we can satisfy our sexual needs without pursuing covenant love. Today, men and women often delay marriage because they have learned to "take care of" their own sexual desires instead of directing those desires toward the pursuit of lifelong love. We also need to consider that masturbation promotes the belief and attitude that sexuality is only for personal pleasure rather than giving love to each other. Some men and women who regularly masturbate find that they have difficulty learning to share their sexuality appropriately once they are married.

3. Aim for maturity.

Many women learned (or were even taught) to masturbate at very young ages. This is particularly true of those who have been sexually violated or "sexualized" in childhood. Sometimes the urge to masturbate is a symptom of deeper issues that need to be addressed.

It may be more effective to address masturbation as an issue of spiritual maturity than an issue of right and wrong. As you grow in your walk with God and as you develop a fuller understanding of His design for sexuality, masturbation will likely become less of an issue. God will give you wisdom that goes beyond the "white knuckle approach" of suppressing sexual desire. More important than the question, "Am I masturbating?" you may want to ask, "How am I moving toward God's design for my sexuality?"

Have you ever really thought about what it means to be the temple of the Holy Spirit?

What does 1 Corinthians 6:12–20 say about the importance of our bodies as followers of Jesus?

How does sexual immorality keep you from sexual wholeness?

HOW DO I FLEE SEXUAL IMMORALITY?

Maybe you are convinced that hookups, lust, fantasy, and porn are bad solutions to your loneliness and longings, but you still feel stuck in a cycle of sin. How do you get "unstuck"? As you've been reading the past few weeks, fleeing temptation is not only what you do in the moment when you feel tempted, it is also learning why you are drawn to sexual immorality.

Sexual sin presents an illegitimate way to address legitimate needs and desires. This is why your freedom journey involves so much more than willpower. To let go of your current coping strategies, you have to also be building new ways of addressing your true needs and desires. Learning to "flee" sin is a lifelong process, but one that you can take steps in right now. The Bible tells us that God always provides a "way of escape" (1 Cor. 10:13 ESV) when we are tempted to sin. That escape hatch might look like literally running away from a situation, breaking off a relationship, getting rid of your smartphone, or calling a friend for prayer and help.

Learning to flee also requires us to remove temptations in advance. If it is a person who tempts you—don't spend alone time with them. If it is sexual scenes in movies or

TV shows—don't watch them. If it is your computer or phone—leave it in a public room of the house. For me (Joy), this looked like removing any media that triggered me to turn back to porn.

What specific step can you take to remove temptation from your life?

Next time you are tempted, flee. Do whatever you can to run from the situation and experience the freedom that God has promised you. Even before the moment of temptation, it is wise to already have a place of action for how you will respond when you are tempted.

There's nothing sinful about encountering temptation. What truly matters is what you do with that temptation.

In moments of temptation, remember to turn to the Spirit of God for help. Ask the Lord to give you His strength and thoughts. Remember, your journey to healing and freedom is a process—it doesn't usually happen overnight.

God loves you so much and does not want you to be chained to sexual sins. Ask the Holy Spirit to remind you the next time you are tempted that there is another way out. Do whatever you can to run from the situation and experience the freedom that God provides.

Because of the addictive elements of sexual sin, it might take time to die to your passions and for the fruit of the Holy Spirit to develop in your life. Friend, we are all on a journey toward sexual integrity. You will experience freedom as you make the daily choice to believe that "you were washed, you were sanctified, you were justified in the name of the Lord Jesus Christ and by the Spirit of our God" (1 Cor. 6:11).

Sexual Wholeness in Marriage and Singleness

In Day 2, you learned about how important it is to begin with embracing your new identity in Christ. Sexual integrity means living based on that new identity in Christ Jesus. The power to *do* differently comes from the truth that we *are* different. As a child of God, your view of sex will begin to change. Maybe you used to think of sex between two consenting adults as perfectly moral behavior. But as a follower of God, you will begin to embrace a new understanding of sex.

Today, we will pick up right where we left off in 1 Corinthians. Paul continues his teaching on sex by specifically addressing what sexual integrity looks like for both the married and the single Christian.

Today will be a brief overview of sexual integrity applied to marriage and to singleness. However, at Authentic Intimacy, we have many follow-up resources that will go much deeper in the application of these principles. You might want to check out resources like *Sex and the Single Girl* and *God, Sex, and Your Marriage,* in addition to podcasts and blogs that speak directly to many of the questions with which you might be wrestling.

SEXUAL WHOLENESS AND MARRIAGE

Read 1 Corinthians 7:1–5. Paul addresses the place of sexual intimacy within marriage.

Let me warn you, these verses are often misrepresented and misinterpreted in ways that have caused confusion for married women. Since this book isn't about marriage, here are the basics you need to understand from this passage:

- If you are a married Christian, your body not only belongs to you and God, but also to your spouse. This means that you strive to make sexual decisions that honor God and your spouse.

- Sexual intimacy in marriage is powerful and important. Both the husband and wife should prioritize and pursue sexual intimacy in marriage.

- Sexual intimacy is designed to be mutual. Both the husband's and wife's drives, desires, and journeys are important.

God created sexual intimacy as a physical sign of the covenant promise a husband and wife make to each other in marriage. With their bodies, a man and woman remember their promise to give themselves to one another. The physical intimacy between a husband and wife is a sacred symbol of their promise.

As married women, we will tell you that living with sexual integrity in marriage can be just as challenging as it was as a single person. The struggle may be different, but it is still real. Getting married doesn't solve all of your sexual problems—even a struggle with porn. It doesn't erase temptations. In some ways, it can create new ones. Married and unmarried Christians have to learn to steward their sexuality in a way that honors their spouse and God.

Have you ever considered that sexual integrity is not only what we say no to, but also what we say yes to?

Have you ever believed the lie that marriage will fix your sexual sin struggles? If so, how does it feel now reading that this isn't true?

SEXUAL WHOLENESS AND SINGLENESS

The rest of Paul's teaching on sexual wholeness may surprise you. While he spends five verses on sex and marriage, he writes about four times more about the importance and beauty of being a single Christian. Take a look in your Bible at 1 Corinthians 7:6–39.

Here are some key points from Paul's teaching in this passage:

- If you are married, you should not seek to be single. Honor your marriage covenant.

- Don't believe that Christian maturity comes through marriage. Both marriage and singleness are gifts from God. Paul's opinion is that it is even better to be single than to be married.

- Remaining unmarried can save you from the challenges of being married, freeing you to be more devoted to God and to His kingdom.

You may have grown up believing that to be sexually whole, you need to be married. This is not true! Paul is saying that marriage is a gift from God, but so is singleness. He writes that he wishes many more Christians could be like he was: unmarried, fulfilled, and devoted to knowing and serving God.

How is Paul's explanation of sexual wholeness different than you would have defined it?

It may be easier for you to imagine what being married and sexually whole looks like because married women get to have sex. Unfortunately, most single Christian women have gotten very little direction on what it practically looks like to live with sexual integrity (other than "don't have sex . . ."): Here are some of the most important things for you to know.

1. Sexual wholeness is not about having a great sex life.
It means understanding, embracing and living according to God's design for sexuality. Some unmarried women are more "sexually whole" than many married women.

Our friend Tamara shares what this looked like for her to pursue sexual wholeness as a single woman:

For a long time, I believed that my sexuality only made sense in the context of marriage that I was waiting and hoping for. As the years passed and I didn't get married, I had to reconsider what it means to be a sexual being as a single person/woman. I embarked on a journey of discovering how to steward my sexuality in a way that is God-honoring and consistent with my values and beliefs instead of it being motivated by the reward of the future marriage and great sex life. Getting a better understanding of what it means to be created as a sexual being; reading different books on the topic of sexuality and singleness; having conversations with my other unmarried friends on this topic; lamenting to God about my expectations and hopes for sexual fulfillment in marriage that wasn't happening; and letting go of the promises God never made—were really crucial steps on the journey of pursuing sexual wholeness in my singleness. Additionally, being pickier on my media intake (movies, books, social media, etc.), giving and receiving appropriate physical affection from my friends and family, as well as moving my body through exercise and dancing were some of the practical ways to embrace and steward my sexuality. I also realized that there is more to intimacy than physical sex. Being emotionally vulnerable and sharing my victories and struggles with close friends and family members, as well as coming to God in prayer, helps me to feel connected and known by others.

Marriage and sex were not created to save you or complete you. Only God can do that. The "finish line" of sexual integrity is not marriage! The finish line, instead, is living a life that puts God above everything else. You don't need sex, but you do need intimacy. In our culture, your real needs for connection, to be loved and known, are often channeled into what you experience as sexual needs.

2. God created you as a sexual person and said that was good!

Being a sexual woman does not necessarily mean you are having sex. Everyone, by God's design, is a sexual creature regardless of age, marital status, or sexual desire. To be sexual means that you are a gendered person (male or female) and you have the capacity to experience longings for intimacy, closeness, and sexual expression. You don't become sexual when you get married. Instead, you work on awakening and channeling those desires as an expression of your marriage covenant.

Our late friend, Dr. Doug Rosenau, described that in addition to our capacity for "genital sexuality," we are also socially sexual people.[2] You bring your sexuality with you everywhere you go. Sexual integrity doesn't mean denying or shutting down your sexual self. It means stewarding your femininity, your desires, and your longings based on your current life circumstances as a single woman.

3. God created sex to be a celebration of the covenant promise of marriage.
Imagine for a moment that you told everyone that today was your birthday. Your friends brought you a cake, took you out for a special dinner, and gave you gifts. The problem is that today is not really your birthday. You just wanted to pretend that it was so you would feel special. What's wrong with this picture?

While there is nothing wrong with celebrating a birthday, the celebration would lack integrity if it wasn't your true birthday. You would be celebrating something that isn't true. This same principle applies to sex outside of the marriage covenant. While sexual intimacy is a good thing, it lacks integrity if it is not the celebration of the covenant vows of marriage. This is why Paul tells married people to work on sexual intimacy, but tells singles to honor God by abstaining from sex.

What one specific thing did you learn about sexual integrity that you can start applying today?

We Are All Sexually Broken

When I (Joy) was single, I worried about what the conversation would look like when I told a boyfriend about my story and my passion to talk about it. Honestly, I doubted a guy would want to stay with me once he realized I previously watched porn and now publicly talk about it.

My husband and I met on an elevator. We both had moved to Dallas, Texas, to attend Dallas Theological Seminary. Early in our friendship, we were driving to visit a new church on a Sunday.

Zack casually said, "I read your blog. You have such a passion to help women."

I responded, "Which ones did you read?"

"All of them."

Picture yourself in my shoes. I've known this guy for a few weeks. I'm beginning to think maybe we could possibly have something starting and he tells me he had read every blog I had ever written? I was overwhelmed, but also relieved that I didn't have to audibly share my story with him. He knew my story, yet he wasn't treating me any differently. He still smiled at me and laughed at my jokes. There was no judgment or shock. His eyes looked at me like Jesus looks at me — with purity, love, and passion.

A few weeks later, we went out for coffee, and I said to him, "You know everything about me. Tell me about you." I learned that my husband had never struggled with porn.

When we started dating, I believed I was a worse sinner, more sexually broken, and a stumbling block in my relationship with Zack. The shame I felt crept into our relationship. It didn't matter how much Zack said that he loved me or saw me as pure, I always felt like I was the worst sinner, until I read a quote from Juli that stopped me in my tracks: *We are all sexually broken.*

As I processed this thought, I began to understand and really believe that, although our stories were different, we were both sinners. Zack brought his own sexual brokenness to our relationship, even if it didn't look like mine.

Jesus said, "You have heard that it was said, 'You shall not commit adultery.' But I tell you that anyone who looks at a woman lustfully has already committed adultery with her in his heart" (Matt. 5:27–28). For some reason, the church has historically labeled this sexual sin as the "worst sin." Sadly, this causes a lot of brothers and sisters in Christ to feel worthless and even walk away from the church. Jesus challenged this belief. Jesus' teaching explains that even lusting or thinking about a person sexually who is not your spouse comes from the same heart as committing adultery.

Have you ever felt like you were more sexually broken than someone else?

If so, how has believing this lie influenced your friendships and relationships?

HOW WE BECAME "BROKEN"

The phrase "sexual brokenness" might feel offensive to some people. It doesn't feel good to be labeled as broken. But the truth is, we can't seek wholeness until we acknowledge that something is broken.

Zack's journey was different from mine. Yours is also unique, but for all of us, there are four major contributors to our state of being sexually broken:

1. We are sinners. (See Rom. 8:7–8 and Eph. 2:1–3)
Sin is not just something we do, it is also part of our fallen nature. The Bible tells us the bad news that all of our thoughts are twisted by evil, even from birth. This means that, without God's help, we will naturally think about sex as something to be consumed rather than as a celebration of covenant.

2. We live in a fallen world. (See Rom. 8:19–21)

Some of our sexual brokenness results from the fact that this world is not what it was originally created to be. From birth, our bodies can experience deformity and brokenness that have nothing to do with our personal sin. The brokenness of this world also means that we will have deep longings and needs that won't be fulfilled on this side of heaven.

3. We are impacted by the sin of others. (See Luke 17:1–2)

At some level, we have all been sexually wounded by other people. You were sexually harmed by the person who introduced you to porn and the person who created the porn. In my story, I (Joy) was also sexually wounded by the guy who date-raped me. We can be deeply harmed by the sin of other people, for decades carrying with us brokenness inflicted by others.

4. Satan works against holiness. (See Matt. 4:1–11)

Finally, sexuality is a spiritual battlefield. God's enemy, Satan, hates everything holy, including the beauty of holy sexuality. Satan can't make you sin, but he does exploit your weaknesses. His ultimate goal is not simply to add to your sexual brokenness, but to separate you from God's love. How many have walked away from faith in God because of the sexual pain and shame they have experienced?

In what ways has your own sin contributed to your sexual brokenness?

In what ways has living in a fallen world contributed to your sexual brokenness?

In what ways has the sin of others contributed to your sexual brokenness?

How does Satan use your sexual brokenness to keep you from the love of God?

WHY OUR SEXUAL BROKENNESS MATTERS

When you hear that "we are all sexually broken" that might make you feel content to stay right where you are. If you are just like everyone else, what's the big deal? Why do the hard work of healing?

I learned from Juli that "every sexual issue is a spiritual issue." Our sexual brokenness is not just about our sexuality, it is also a spiritual issue. In the recovery journey, we discover our porn problem is directly connected to what we believe about God. Our sexuality and our spirituality cannot be separated into separate categories.

Underneath my struggle with porn was a girl who longed to feel loved by her heavenly Father. I didn't know that God's love was more than enough to meet my desire for deep intimate connection. I also longed to be comforted from the pain I went through from my sexual trauma.

You may turn to porn for comfort, not realizing the pleasure from porn only lasts a few seconds while the comfort of God lasts into eternity. You can have multiple spiritual longings that porn will never come close to fixing. Your freedom journey is so critical because your sexual issues can never be separated from your spiritual life. As Juli often says, "When sex becomes confusing, God becomes confusing." Your struggle with lust, pornography, shame, and your longing to be loved are all part of your relationship with God. Sexual bondage will also mean spiritual bondage.

Take a few minutes to think about what your spiritual issues might be, then list them below. (Examples: not trusting God, not knowing His intimate love, and not understanding God's design for sexuality or the role of the Holy Spirit in our life and freedom journey).

Our journey toward sexual wholeness requires daily surrendering to God. The truth is our hearts are divided instead of wholly surrendered to Him (remember integrity!). We are human and torn between the desires of the flesh and the desires of the spirit. Wholeness means that we are daily asking God to unite more pieces of our heart toward His design, to be more under the control of the Holy Spirit. It is a daily (sometimes hourly!) conversation and exchange between you and God, where you present to Him your mess and invite His presence into that place.

In 1 Thessalonians 5:23, Paul writes, "Now may the God of peace himself sanctify you completely, and may your whole spirit and soul and body be kept blameless at the coming of our Lord Jesus Christ" (ESV). Notice the words "completely" and "whole spirit and soul and body." God Himself is the one who sanctifies us completely.

As we end this week, consider this:

If this heart represents your sexuality, color in the percentage that has fully been surrendered to God. Identify areas that are yet to be reclaimed. Write down the things that are still covered in shame, pain, or confusion. There is power in naming and bringing our struggles into the light.

If there are still parts that feel divided, name those parts of your heart that have not been surrendered to the Lord.

WEEK 3: SMALL GROUP DISCUSSION QUESTIONS

1. What why questions do you have about God and sex? How have your why questions been ignored rather than explored or encouraged?

2. Do you believe God cares about your sexuality? Why or why not?

3. How are you allowing your past sexual sin or current struggle to continue to define you?

4. How would you describe the difference between seeking sexual purity and sexual integrity?

5. Why is it so important to understand that purity comes from God and not our own works?

6. Do you believe it is possible to be sexually whole as a single Christian? Why or why not?

7. Have you ever felt like you were more sexually broken than someone else? If so, how has believing this lie influenced your friendships and relationships?

8. Share your colored-in heart images with your group. How much of your heart is wholly surrendered to the Lord? Which parts are surrendered? Which parts are you holding back from Him?

Pursuing Sexual Integrity

The past three weeks, you've been learning a different way to view your struggle with porn and a different paradigm of sexual wholeness. Maybe you are getting frustrated because we haven't given you a ton of practical things to do differently in your battle with sexual sin. I (Juli) have learned that you can't *do* sex differently until you *think* about it differently. Changes in behavior begin with changes in perspective and priority.

Now it's time to begin practically applying what you have been learning.

You are on a journey to move from sexual brokenness to wholeness, from bondage to freedom. Remember, this is a freedom *journey*, not a sprint. If you want to run a marathon, you train for months, sometimes even years. You begin with a decision (I'm going to run a marathon), followed by small steps (I'm going to start training tomorrow). Most people can't just jump off the couch and run a marathon. Have you ever heard of the Couch to 5K training plan? It's a plan to train people to run long distances over time. Likewise, the process of becoming more like Christ is also a journey.

Your journey begins with the choice to believe in God and to walk in His light every day. The more you walk in the light, the more you will look like Christ and the less you will desire your old ways of sin.

Come Out of Hiding

Have you ever been in a dark space for hours and then it's suddenly flooded with light? In that moment, light doesn't feel like a blessing. It overloads your senses, making you squint until your eyes can adjust.

While light helps us see and navigate the world, we may not initially welcome it.

Maybe that's how you have felt diving into this book. What will God ask you to reveal? What will He show you about yourself?

I (Joy) remember that fear. The enemy had me in darkness for months with my secret addiction to pornography. I was a new Christian and excited about God. But I had a secret compartment in my life that I didn't know how to deal with. I wanted to honor God, but couldn't stop sinning. For months, I lived in this secrecy, afraid to tell anyone because I had never heard a Christian talk about porn, especially in regard to women. It was eating away at me.

Knowing Jesus is all about stepping into the light. The Bible says that He not only *brings* light, He *is* light. Sometimes that light feels like the warmth of sunshine and the clarity of seeing things as they are. But for me in that season, the light of Jesus felt like a heavy weight. The closer I drew to Jesus, the more I felt sapped by my secret sin. I thought about telling someone but was so afraid to be exposed. *What if they judge me or reject me? What if no guy ever wants to date me?*

Sexual sin and struggles have a unique way of keeping us in the darkness. We begin to believe that no one—not even God—would love us if they really knew the truth. I believed that lie for many years. It's easier to keep your sin a secret, wrapped up in the darkness of your mind. It's easier to minimize your struggle or rationalize the sin you find yourself constantly falling into. The enemy sets up strongholds in your secrets. As you begin to step into the light, you invite God to begin His healing work of cleaning out your sin and cleansing your heart. Stepping out of the darkness was not easy, but it radically changed my life.

The light of Jesus may make you feel uncomfortable at first, convicting you of sin, but the purpose of His light is freedom. "For God did not send his Son into the world to condemn the world, but to save the world through him" (John 3:17). Part of your journey to freedom includes learning to walk in the light.

God doesn't want us to hide *from* Him. Instead, He invites us to hide *in* Him. God knows us inside and out, "For you [God] created my inmost being; you knit me together in my mother's womb" (Ps. 139:13). He knows our secrets and our sins, and yet He loves us so much that He still chose to die for us. We only experience freedom as we walk toward Him. As I have grown in my relationship with God, this has become my reality and has proven to provide the only comfort that is lasting.

Psalm 32 is a beautiful song, showing us the choice we need to make to hide *in* God instead of *from* Him.

Read Psalm 32:1–2. What does David say will happen to us when we run to God with our sin and shame?

Read Psalm 32:3–4. What happened to David when he hid his sin from God? Have you ever felt like this?

Read Psalm 32:5. What step did David take to "come out of hiding"? What was God's response?

I was a freshman in college, in a different state, without friends, and God used my pain and loneliness to lead me to Him. At my lowest point, I went to Cru, a college ministry, and heard the story of God's grace. Right there, I surrendered my life to Jesus and trusted that He could heal me from my wounds and shame.

I spent my days and nights lying in bed, crying out to God for answers. I began reading the Bible, God's love letters, for the first time. I learned that God loved me, and I didn't have to earn His love by being perfect. Before that moment, I was lost, "hiding" in relationships in an attempt to fill my emptiness. My whole life, I had gone to church, but I lacked a personal relationship with Jesus. I didn't know what it meant to "hide in God." I went to church, but I did not intimately know Jesus.

List some of the ways you have tried to hide from your fear, pain, and shame.

Read Psalm 32:6–7. What does David tell us to do? What does David say that God will do when we hide in Him?

What would it look like for you to run to God as your hiding place right now?

Read Psalm 32:5–11. How does God minister to us when we hide in Him?

There is great power in not only stepping into the light of God's love, but then trusting His love enough to be willing to reach out for help. I promise life is better when you step out of darkness and into the light. You can never heal in hiding. Hiding might feel safe in the moment, but it kills you in the long run. You have a choice right now to hide from God (in your normal hiding places) or to choose to make God your hiding place.

Don't put this off. Right now is the perfect time for you to come out of hiding! Here's how . . .

1. Be honest with God about your sin, your doubts, and your feelings.

2. Confess to God the ways you have hidden from Him in the past.

3. Ask God to teach you to learn to hide *in* Him instead of hiding *from* Him.

Find Your People

Coming out of hiding begins with confessing your sin to God, but it doesn't end there. In James 5:16, we learn that part of our healing journey is to "confess our sins to one another." You may find that it's easier to tell God what you are struggling with (after all, He already knows!) than to be honest with another human being.

Once we invite God into our struggles, we need to then invite others in as well. It can be tempting to address sexual sin with just you and God, but that allows you to still stay in hiding. When I refused to invite anyone else in to help me with my sexual struggles, I was trying to fight temptations in my own strength alone. This got me nowhere, and I found myself alone in my room each night watching more and more porn for longer periods of time—resulting in more self-hatred.

After many failed attempts at stopping my addiction on my own, I reached out to a safe person at my church and began meeting with her weekly. The more I stepped into the light, the more I wanted to find freedom and stop hiding. At one point, I took a pretty drastic step! I like to call this my "doorknob moment." After many nights of stumbling, I decided to remove the doorknob from my bedroom door. At the time, I was living in a condo with five other girls. I had my own room and was struggling with porn almost daily. I had finally gotten to a place where I would do anything to find freedom. My door was allowing me to physically hide my sin and struggle. So, I found a screwdriver and removed the doorknob from my door.[1]

The day after I removed it, my roommates were confused. One friend simply asked, "Why does your door not have a doorknob?" Another one asked, "Will our landlord be upset?" Both questions resulted in me confessing my secrets, which actually started to create a space for openness and accountability for all of us in our home.

What are your fears about seeking accountability?

What kind of "doorknob" decision could you make?

What step of accountability might you need to take to invite freedom into your life?

Years later, I now have accountability software on my devices, a trusted counselor, and friends I lean on. Many nights I've lain in bed, unable to sleep, and the temptation to look at porn has crept into my mind. As a Christian leader in ministry, I want to hold myself to a high level of accountability. Just knowing that my best friend and husband would be notified if I look at anything on my devices keeps me from clicking.

Will accountability software solve my porn problem?

Accountability software won't cure you of your addiction, and the software may not effectively filter things such as erotica in the form of words. However, it can be one of the tools you use on your journey. Dominique, a woman who tried this tool, said having a friend hold her accountable was far more helpful. Dominique's friend would ask tough questions that led Dominique into an open and honest conversation about her actions and habits that week.

> A combination of strategies can be effective—the key is accountability. Marnie Ferree, a leader in the field of sexual addiction, believes accountability is "one of the key foundation blocks of a strong recovery."[2] She says that "effective accountability is something you invite into your life . . . if you don't choose it, you'll ultimately defy it."[3]

ACCOUNTABILITY IS KEY

Second Timothy 2:22 says, "Flee the evil desires of youth and pursue righteousness, faith, love and peace, along with those who call on the Lord out of a pure heart." We usually focus on the word *flee* in this verse. While fleeing sin is important, I want you to look at the phrase "with those." We can't flee alone. We can't go through recovery alone—we need one another.

Ava found freedom and hope through an accountability partner at church. "Having someone to talk to and be with me on my journey of recovery is amazing," she said. "I was also able to find a support group at one of my local churches for women who [are addicted to porn or sexual relationships]. I'm still healing, and my progress isn't perfect, but I'm growing. I have never regretted my decision to confess about my addiction."[4]

You might feel encouraged by stories like mine or others shared here, but you don't know where to start in finding people to invite into your journey. Confessing sexual sin to another person is terrifying. I know. I was there. Maybe you've tried to confess to someone in the past and they shut you down or responded with judgment. It might take time to discover people who will walk with you on your journey toward freedom and integrity. Some accountability relationships are friendships, and others take the form of mentors or counselors. Both types of relationships are important.

Read Hebrews 10:24–25 and Ecclesiastes 4:10. What do these verses teach us about accountability relationships?

ACCOUNTABILITY IN WISE COUNSELORS

In the Bible, we read about Paul's relationship with Timothy. Paul was Timothy's "spiritual father," who encouraged and challenged him in his walk with the Lord. Throughout your life, you need mentors and wise counselors to advise you. This can take the form of an informal discipleship relationship or a licensed professional counselor.

Here's the catch—you are going to have to seek this out. No counselor will call you. It's very unlikely that someone will ask to mentor you. God will place opportunities and people around you but you are going to have to intentionally pray, seek, and ask for an older, wiser person to become a "Paul" to you.

The book of Proverbs gives us at least seven traits of a wise counselor:

1. A wise counselor fears the Lord. (9:10)

2. A wise counselor has a good reputation. (22:1)

3. A wise counselor is willing to "wound you" when you need to hear difficult truths. (27:6)

4. A wise counselor encourages a team of people in your life who will provide wisdom. (15:22)

5. A wise counselor speaks words that give life and encouragement. (1:8)

6. A wise counselor has spent time studying and learning. (1:7)

7. A wise counselor knows the limits of human wisdom and will point you to God Himself. (20:24)

As you look through this list of qualities, write down the name of a person or two you know who would be a wise counselor. If you are unable to find a specific person, begin praying for God to lead you to the right person.

Read Proverbs 4:1–7. What does this passage say is your role in seeking wisdom?

ACCOUNTABILITY IN COMMUNITY AND FRIENDSHIP

Unlike a mentor or counseling relationship, accountability friendships include mutual sharing, vulnerability, and willingness to confront. Proverbs says, "As iron sharpens iron, so one person sharpens another" (27:17). These are friends who agree to walk in the light together and to hold each other accountable to God's standards for their lives. These relationships include meeting regularly, sharing aspects of your spiritual journey, and pursuing God together. You can check in on how you're doing in your walk with God by asking questions like, "How is your time with God? What are you reading in the Bible?" These questions aren't to make you feel ashamed of your struggles, but to help you see where you are spiritually, where you have room to grow, and where a friend can join beside you to help you thrive.

Having a safe person or small group to talk with is key to finding freedom. A safe person is someone you feel comfortable sharing and being vulnerable with, someone who doesn't gossip, and someone who has the same commitment to follow Jesus.

Confession and prayer should be a regular part of your accountability relationships. These relationships can also become the people you reach out to in the middle of temptation.

This type of friend or group will support you through hard times, help you wrestle with specific sins, ask you how you are doing, pray for you, and speak God's truth to you in love. Building safe and vulnerable relationships like this may take time, but it's worth it. You may actually be going through this book with a friend or group of friends who can develop into accountability relationships.

Read 1 Corinthians 10:13. What does this passage say about what God will provide when you are tempted?

How might calling or texting an accountability partner be a "way of escape" (1 Cor. 10:13 ESV) the next time you face sexual temptation?

Write down the names of two people who can become your accountability friends. If no one comes to mind, you could join an online small group to find other like-minded women. At Authentic Intimacy, we offer Online Book Studies multiple times per year.

Identifying Your Triggers

Getting to the real problem beneath your porn problem often begins with learning to identify triggers. Triggers are things happening around you that tap into an emotion, memory, or learned behavior. For example, every time I walk into the kitchen, I want something to eat. Even if I'm not hungry, walking into the kitchen triggers me to open the fridge or cupboard, looking for a snack.

When we turn to sexual sin, we are often reacting to a trigger we feel or experience. Triggers can be emotions or feelings, common situations, or memories from the past. There are some feelings (like loneliness) or experiences (like being ignored by a guy you like) that trigger you to seek comfort through porn.

BIOLOGICAL TRIGGERS

As women, we have sexual desires and sexual hormones that can heighten temptation to look at porn or seek a sexual outlet. During your menstrual cycle, your hormones are constantly fluctuating. About midway through your cycle, or when you ovulate, you are more likely to desire sex because your body is doing what it was designed to do—release an egg to produce a baby. This is when female bodies produce more estrogen and testosterone, which can increase your sex drive.[5]

If you feel more "sexual" at certain times of the month, one step to take is to begin tracking your monthly cycle. There are several apps that help you track your cycle and symptoms so you can be prepared. Desiring a sexual release more during certain times of the month is normal. God designed the woman's body with hormones and with sexual desire. We need to learn how to steward and manage these natural hormones and feelings.

Have you discovered that you are more tempted during certain times of the month? If so, how can you prepare ahead of time to be on guard during those dates?

You may also experience sexual temptation when you are hungry or tired. Every few hours we will get hungry, and every evening we will need to go to bed. These natural human experiences make us feel weak and vulnerable. If you have promised yourself never to look at porn again, your willpower will probably begin to fade when you are hungry or tired.

I (Joy) often struggle falling asleep at night, and it is in those moments of tiredness that I have turned to porn in the past. If masturbation and having an orgasm is linked to your porn struggle, you experience a release of endorphins that make you more relaxed and more able to fall asleep. The more regular this habit becomes, the more addictive it becomes as you train your body to need this to fall asleep. If this is something you struggle with, it will be helpful to create a nighttime routine to relax your body and mind. This could include no screen time before bed, reading a book, listening to calming music, or having a relaxing bath.

How have you experienced hunger or tiredness as triggers in your struggle?

EMOTIONAL TRIGGERS

Anger. Sadness. Frustration. Loneliness. These are real feelings, and it's okay to experience them. Instead of feeling our emotions, we often escape them by numbing out through bingeing porn or looking for validation in an unhealthy relationship. What if instead of running from those feelings and hiding in sexual sin, you began to embrace your emotions? Triggers remind us of pain. Porn promises to numb the pain. Healing comes when we address our pain.

This starts with exploring your emotions and being curious about why you feel them.

One way to do this is through journaling. When you experience intense emotions, pause and write down your feelings in a journal. This may help to calm you down and bring clarity to the situation.

Katie realized that moments before watching porn, she often felt upset toward God that she was single. Instead of turning to porn, she started journaling. Katie then recognized that at the heart of her porn struggle was loneliness, sadness and anger. She addressed her need for Christian community by joining a small group of women at her church. Her freedom journey began by sharing her true feelings and struggles with safe Christian friends.

Triggers remind us of pain. Porn promises to numb the pain. Healing comes when we address our pain.

When you experience any type of pain, running to outlets like sexual sin is always easier than entering into the pain—at least in the moment. We know hooking up with another guy won't fix our problems, yet why do we still do it? Even actions we know we shouldn't do, like sending that naked photo or clicking on an image, give us a rush of dopamine that can temporarily numb the pain.

Have you used sexual sin to escape emotions and feelings? If so, which feelings? Did it work, or did the sexual sin only provide a fleeting relief? How did you feel afterward?

Think back on the last time you were tempted to sin sexually. What emotions were you feeling during the moments of temptation?

I (Joy) still experience emotional triggers today and have to decide who or what I will turn to for comfort. Right now, when I feel shameful because of my past or present sins, I turn to food. Ice cream becomes my comfort instead of God. In my moments of shame, when I want to turn to sugar for comfort, these three questions guide me back to "freedom" thinking:

1. What is currently going on in my life that makes me want to turn to something besides God for comfort?

2. What emotions do I feel?

3. Will this earthly thing I turn to provide lasting comfort, or will it last only for a moment?

Next time you experience an emotional trigger, pause and consider these questions. After spending time thinking through the heart of my shame, I ask God for the strength to turn to Him and not to food. Even when I do turn to popsicles, God, in His grace, invites me out of my hiding and into His light.

TRIGGERS AND TEMPTATION

Instead of viewing triggers as a bad thing, it may be helpful to see them as warning lights on the dashboard of your heart. Being triggered reminds us of a need—a need for comfort, healing, love, or safety. Rather than just pushing through temptation and ignoring triggers, God wants us to bring our pain, our loneliness, and our anxiety to Him. When I (Joy) was able to more quickly identify my triggers, I was able to find solutions to my real needs instead of using porn as a temporary fix.

One way to remember how to deal with triggers is through the acronym HALT.[6] HALT stands for hungry, angry, lonely, and tired. These four triggers are normal physical feelings that we experience. However, when you're experiencing one of these four legitimate needs, you're more likely to turn to porn.

In the moments of feeling tempted to turn to porn, ask yourself: Am I hungry, angry, lonely, or tired? Next, consider each and brainstorm ways to meet the real need.

Hungry: What is a healthy snack you can eat in moments of hunger?

Angry: Why do you feel angry? Who do you need to forgive? Maybe you're angry at God wondering why He hasn't taken your struggle away yet. Can you journal your feelings?

Lonely: What friend can you call? Can you plan a coffee hangout for tomorrow?

Tired: Can you take a nap or go on a walk? Sometimes we are actually just bored.

In 2 Corinthians 2, Paul tells us that we don't have to be "outwitted" by Satan's schemes. By recognizing our triggers, we become more prepared to recognize moments of temptation.

Pray and ask the Holy Spirit to reveal your triggers to you. Write down a few situations, locations, or feelings that trigger you turn to sexual temptation.

PUTTING IT INTO PRACTICE

We want to end today with a practical project. In it, you'll use what you have been learning to prepare for temptation. We call this your Toolbox. It contains information and strategies that will help you in moments of temptation. You may put different things in your Toolbox than someone else might. You want to customize it to be most helpful.

In your Toolbox, you will have a list of activities you love to do and could easily do in a moment of struggle. For example, I love getting coffee with a friend, but that isn't something I can always do during the time I'm triggered. You'll also include a list of strategies you can easily implement. For instance, you might include the names of people who can encourage you, spend time with you, and support you.

Processing through HALT will help you create your Toolbox. Each idea you brainstorm to deal with those real needs can be added.

Which of the HALT items in the past have made you feel more vulnerable to sexual temptation?

Below is an example of the Toolbox I've created. You'll also find a blank one to fill out for yourself.

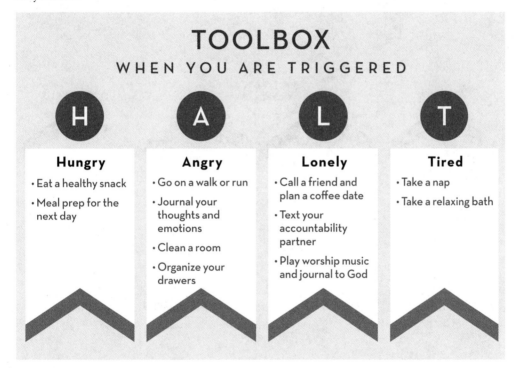

Put your Toolbox somewhere you will see it often. Some women create it in their journal, save it on their phone, or tape it to their bathroom mirror. Spend time now deciding on your tools rather than in a moment of temptation so you are prepared.

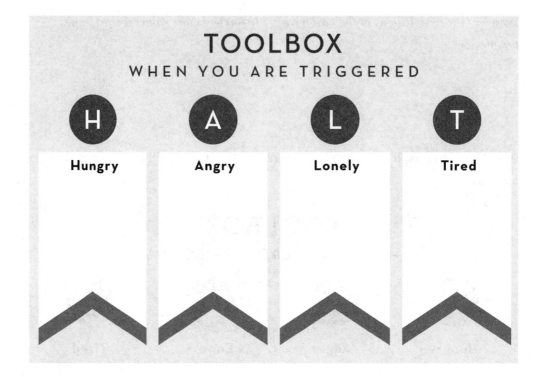

TOOLBOX
WHEN YOU ARE TRIGGERED

H   **A**   **L**   **T**

Hungry   **Angry**   **Lonely**   **Tired**

Get Back Up Again

I (Joy) woke up this morning to a text from my friend Casey that read, "I messed up." Casey shared that she had felt extreme loneliness all day, which led to masturbation. After that, she was scared to fall asleep that night. Casey was filled with shame and couldn't get sexual images from her past out of her brain. After a restless night, Casey decided to take her thoughts captive. She went into the backyard and sat in silence, praying and listening to God. She asked God to remove all the images from her brain.

This was the first time in over a year that Casey had turned back to old habits. But instead of continuing to hide from God and allow her sin to keep her alone in shame, Casey began to actively pursue freedom and healing from the images in her head. The previous year, if Casey had stumbled, it would have sent her down a rabbit hole, bingeing porn for days, but this time she ran to God. Our conversation ended with her texting, "Gotta keep seeking Him!" That's our goal here. God wants our hearts. He wants a relationship with us. We take refuge in God every time we falter, turning toward Him rather than away from Him amid our battle.

If we do turn back to old sin patterns, the quicker we turn back to God and process what happened, the better. If you mess up again and you feel like a failure, do not give up. You may feel like distancing yourself from God, not going to church, or putting the Bible away for a while, but those are all things the enemy desires and not God. He is your safe place. Continuing to run to Him is how we experience lasting freedom.

Think back on the last time you stumbled. How did you respond following the sin? Did you run from God or run to God?

What would look different in your life if you ran to God instead of from God?

Why do you think it is often difficult to seek out God when we sin?

When you believe your worth is found in your sexual choices, you will feel worthless when you fall into sin. These are the moments you need to preach the gospel to your own heart and remember—your worth is not found in your sexuality, but in your identity in Christ. You are a daughter of the King! First John 3:1 states, "See what great love the Father has lavished on us, that we should be called children of God! And that is what we are!"

Where do you get your worth and value—in what Christ says about you or in what others or the world says about you?

How have your sexual choices impacted your feelings of worth?

God is inviting you into a deeper relationship with Him. Hookups, lust, fantasy, porn—whatever you turn to—is a bad solution. Sexual sin might seem to "work" for a season, but eventually it will lead to harm. The Bible tells us, "Do not be deceived: God cannot be mocked. A man reaps what he sows" (Gal. 6:7). You will find nothing good outside of God's will for you.

Jesus is the solution to our problems—He solves our deep need for intimacy. But because of the addictive elements of sexual sin, it might take time to die to our passions and to grow the fruits of the Holy Spirit.

If you experience moments of temptation, don't try to fix yourself and make up for your failure. Instead, turn to the Holy Spirit. Ask God to give you a new mind. It is by His power, forgiveness, and righteousness we can start resisting temptation.

Remember, your journey to healing is a process. Each day you will have many little decisions:

Will I replace these thoughts with God's truth?

Will I choose to watch this sexually explicit show?

Will I share my online activities with an accountability partner?

Will I spend time with God?

List out some other little decisions you could come across each day:

Imagine you have trained for a marathon and today is race day. You start the race strong, but then you trip and fall in the tenth mile. Now you have to decide again—will you get up or go home? Remember, you don't have to start the race over and go back to the starting line. Instead, you can stand up, check for any injuries, maybe take a drink of water, and then get back to running the race. If you're running the marathon with a friend and you trip, they won't just leave you on the ground. They will stop running and lend you a hand. The same should be true of an accountability friend or mentor.

Next time you have a slipup, instead of giving up, kneel and surrender your sexual brokenness to God. Instead of counting the number of days since you last looked at porn, open your Bible and write down a prayer in your journal. Sometimes counting our days since we last sinned can cause discouragement and shame to creep in when we fall into sin.

Freedom from our sexual struggles comes from loving God more, not obeying rules more. We grow in self-control and holiness because of God's grace. We can't earn holiness by what we do or don't do. It's not about trying harder or doing more or being a "good Christian girl"; it's about our personal relationship with Jesus. The more we love Jesus, the more His Spirit gives us self-control and changes our desires to become Christlike. Focus on the relationship, not only on your behavior.

In the book of Matthew, a Pharisee asks Jesus, "'Teacher, which is the greatest commandment in the Law?' Jesus replied: "Love the Lord your God with all your heart and with all your soul and with all your mind." This is the first and greatest commandment'" (22:35–38). Freedom is birthed from loving God, not obeying laws. Once God changes your heart, your behavior will follow. We believe God will not change what we do until He fundamentally changes who we are.

How does it change your approach to know that self-control, as a fruit of the Spirit, grows from loving God more than it does from trying to stop sinning?

To end today's devotional, pray this passage from Ephesians 5 over your day:

> For you were once darkness, but now you are light in the Lord. Live as children of light (for the fruit of the light consists in all goodness, righteousness and truth) and find out what pleases the Lord. Have nothing to do with the fruitless deeds of darkness, but rather expose them. (vv. 8–11)

You, my friend, are a child of the light. May you walk in the light more and more each day.

WEEK 4: SMALL GROUP DISCUSSION QUESTIONS

1. How do you hope sharing with a group can help you come out of hiding?

2. What are some ways sexual sin can affect our real-life relationships with others and with God?

3. On a scale of 0–100 percent, how much do you believe that God cares about your struggles, cries, and pains? How would your sexual struggles look different if you truly believed that God cared 100 percent about your pain and suffering?

4. Share about a time when you chose to hide in God instead of running away from Him. If you've never hidden in God, what would look different if you took this step?

5. What does it look like practically for you to have an accountability partner?

6. Which of the HALT items in the past have made you feel more vulnerable to sexual temptation?

7. Share the items in your Toolbox with the other group members. Brainstorm ideas together. How realistic is it for you to turn to your Toolbox in moments of temptation and do one of the listed activities?

8. Read Philippians 4:8 out loud. What are things you can think about in moments of temptation that are true, noble, right, pure, lovely, admirable, excellent, and praiseworthy?

Ditching Lies and Embracing Truth

To put it bluntly, sexual issues can be downright confusing. We want to trust God's Word, but it seems like culture's take on sex sometimes makes more sense. Your freedom journey involves learning to discern the lies you believe about sexuality, about yourself, and about freedom. As Jesus proclaimed, "The truth will set you free" (John 8:32). That also means that lies will hold you captive. This was true in Tanisha's journey:

> After college, my church stopped talking about singleness and sexuality. It was assumed that you will be married by the time you are in your thirties. Culture was telling me that as a thirty-year-old virgin, I was a "sexually repressed weirdo." I was subjected to shame and embarrassment. I believed that men would question, "Why have you waited for so long?" My struggle has not been

giving in to sexual temptation, but to be rid of the stigma attached to waiting. I began to believe I was missing something important if I'd never had sex.[1] In this short statement, we can see lies that infiltrated Tanisha's thinking. Lies like:

- I should be married by age thirty.
- Virgins are "sexually repressed weirdos."
- To be whole, I should be having sex.
- I should feel ashamed of my virginity.
- Not having sex will make me unlovable.
- Something important in my life will be missing if I don't have sex.

Unfortunately, her church's silence and messaging contributed to the lies Tanisha believed. Beneath every sexual struggle is an undercurrent of lies. Lies might begin in your thoughts, but they don't stay there. In time, they flow over into your beliefs, emotions, and actions.

Because of this, we want to spend this week helping you identify the lies you believe and more importantly, learn to confront those lies with the power of God's truth. First, we want to warn you of two things:

1. This week might be challenging for you. It's not easy to examine the lies we believe. As you will learn, sometimes lies feel more comfortable than the truth.

2. The journey toward truth is a spiritual battle. The father of all lies, Satan, does not want you to expose lies and embrace truth. Ask your friends and fellow group members to pray for you as you go through this week's content. You might also consider some form of fasting this week, asking God for His truth and strength.

Where Do Lies Come From?

I (Joy) can remember believing lies as early as fifth grade. The cute boys didn't like me, but they liked the other girls. I began to believe: *I must not be beautiful.* My young brain took this lie and ran with it. Speaking of running, once I got into high school, I got the message that I could become more attractive by working out. I tried to lose weight so I could gain approval, because I thought losing weight would get me a boyfriend. This played into another lie: *I need a guy to make me feel beautiful.*

What seemed like a simple lie spiraled over time into a web of lies that led to fear and anxiety. Over time, this web of lies became so much a part of my thinking that it felt like the truth. Eventually, I acted out of those lies in my relationships.

Where did these lies come from? Cultural messages through movies, music, and media. What people said to me. Whether or not someone showed me love or affection.

While those are all sources of deception, there is a more powerful, darker source of the lies we believe. You may hear people talk about a "spiritual battle" between good and evil. One very tangible way to understand this battle is to frame it as a war between truth and lies.

THE BATTLE OF TRUTH AND LIES

The Bible clearly tells us that lies come from Satan.

Read John 8:43–44. What does this passage tell you about the source of lies?

What are some lies Satan has spoken to you in the past?

The Bible is equally clear that Jesus Christ represents all truth. Jesus Himself said, "I am the way and the truth and the life" (John 14:6). Did you get that? Jesus didn't just say that He *speaks* truth but that He *is* truth.

Why do you think Jesus said, "I am the truth" not just "I speak truth"?

The battle between truth and lies is not just a war between two separate ways of thinking, but is rooted in who we will ultimately believe. Do we believe God or do we believe Satan? Satan is always looking for ways to reinforce lies. Why? Because he knows that when we believe lies, we are naturally separated from the truth of God's Word and His love. Even though we have likely never personally met you, we are confident that your battle with pornography involves a battle between truth and lies.

In many ways, your growth and maturity as a godly woman is the ongoing exchange of lies for truth. This is why it is so important for you to spend time in God's Word, nurture friendships with people who remind you of truth, and also why it may be important for you to be thoughtful about how your past impacts how you currently think about things.

Both of us are committed to this process in our own lives. That is why it is so important to find the root of the lies we believe. For me (Joy), the root lie I believed was that I was unloved, even unlovable. None of the things I ran to could fill the void in my heart to feel beautiful and loved. Unfortunately, I learned this the hard and painful way.

The only thing that could set me free from that lie was to cling to the truth of God's love. He took my broken, lie-believing self and helped me realize that only He can heal me and love me the way I need to be loved.

Whatever lie or lies are at the root of your struggle, you have a Father who loves you. You have a Savior who died to set you free. God sent the Holy Spirit to help you recognize the lies you believe.

Read John 16:13. Who does this verse say will lead you into truth?

How does it make you feel to know that the Holy Spirit will lead you to truth?

Write a prayer, asking God over the next few days to show you specific lies you have been believing.

The Four Biggies, Part 1

It doesn't feel good to realize that you might be believing lies. Here's the good news—through God's Word, we have a sneak peek at Satan's lie "manual."

Satan has been lying to human beings since the very beginning. You probably know the story . . . Satan tempted Eve to eat the fruit of the tree of the knowledge of good and evil. Once she did, she shared it with Adam, who also chose to go against God's command. While this might sound like an ancient tale, it actually gives us a good understanding into how God's enemy, Satan, uses lies to entice people into sin.

Over the next two days, we are going to look at Genesis 3:1–6.

Read Genesis 3:1–6. Satan is described as crafty. What do you think that means? What does this tell you about him?

SATAN'S BIG LIE #1 — YOU CAN'T TRUST GOD'S WORD

As Satan talked with Eve, he began with this question: "Did God really say, 'You must not eat from any tree in the garden'?" Gen. 3:1).

With this question, Satan introduced doubt about the trustworthiness of God (did He *really* say…?). What had seemed so clear and obvious now became murky for Eve.

There is a lot of confusion and doubt about what God has said about sex. *Did God really say sex is only for marriage? Sex is such a personal issue, does God really care about my sexual choices?*

This confusion isn't a random evolution of culture. Satan wants you to be confused about right and wrong. God has a will for your sex life. He has been very clear about what it looks like to honor Him with your sexuality, but that clarity can so easily get caught in a web of lies.

You might believe: *God is okay with me looking at porn.*

Women who are struggling with sexual sin, specifically pornography, often ask, "Why is porn wrong? Is it really a sin to watch porn?" In other words, *Did God really say?*

As you learned earlier, God created sex to be intrinsically tied to covenant love. Jesus was clear in Matthew 5:28 that sexual immorality is not only what we do with our bodies, but what we do with our thoughts.

Instead of embracing God's truth and will for our lives, it's easy to rationalize.

What's the big deal? At least I'm not sleeping around.
I'm so good in every other area of life. This is just my one issue.
No one is going to know.
I deserve this. I've had a really tough week.
I'm unmarried. I'll stop when I get engaged.

I've heard all of these statements used to justify porn use. Maybe you've had these same thoughts or similar ones.

Take a look at the list of statements above. Circle any of them that you have thought or said before related to your porn use.

How has Satan's lies confused you about God's design for your sex life?

When did you first begin to believe those lies?

Not only did Satan cause Eve to doubt by asking "Did God really say. . .?" he added to the doubt by ever so slightly changing God's original command.

Read Genesis 2:16–17. Now read Genesis 3:1. How is Satan's statement different from God's command to Adam and Eve?

What does this show you about Satan's strategy?

Satan not only wants you to think that porn is okay, but that God is anti-sex.

You might believe: *Sex is bad! My sexuality itself is shameful.*

The truth is that God created sex and He said it was very good. One book in the Bible, Song of Solomon, is filled with references to a sexual relationship within the commitment of marriage. Just look at the first few verses, "Let him kiss me with the kisses of his mouth — for your love is more delightful than wine. Pleasing is the fragrance of your perfumes; your name is like perfume poured out. No wonder the young women love you! Take me away with you — let us hurry! Let the king bring me into his chambers" (1:1–4).

On a scale from 1 to 10 (1, not at all; 10, a lot!), how strongly have you believed the lie that sex is bad or that God doesn't care about your sexuality?

Why do you think Satan wants you to believe this?

How has believing this lie impacted your struggle with pornography? Your relationship with God?

SATAN'S BIG LIE #2 — NOTHING BAD WILL HAPPEN

As you continue reading what happened between Eve and Satan, you will notice a second big lie. This one is found in Genesis 3:3. God said that if Adam and Eve ate of the tree in the center of the garden, they would die. Satan responded, "You will not certainly die" (v. 4). Satan wants you to believe that there are no true consequences to sin. Maybe God won't be happy with you, but He will forgive you. Sin is no big deal.

We have seen this play out in responding to temptation. Here are a few versions of the lies you may begin to believe:

You might believe: *Porn doesn't affect me.*

The truth is that porn does impact you. It interferes with your relationship with God, and it teaches you a self-centered approach to sexuality. When you lust, watch porn, or masturbate, you make sexuality all about you. This focus doesn't go away if you get married. You have essentially trained yourself to respond sexually only to your own thoughts and your own touch.

Pornography also trains you to look at people as objects for your pleasure rather than as people made in God's image.

Porn becomes your sex education, creating false expectations. The sex displayed on the screen is nothing like sex in real life. The people acting in porn are edited and photoshopped, and the women are usually struggling with eating disorders. Watching photoshopped women have sex on the screen creates body image issues because you think you need to look like them, without realizing that what you are looking at is fake.

Ironically, porn itself is one big lie. Porn is fake—portraying sex completely devoid of love and intimacy. When you consume fake sex, you begin to think that real sex will look the same way. Looking at porn or media as your sex education sets you up for disappointment when married sex looks nothing like the fake sex you've been consuming.

Porn teaches us that sex is easy and perfect. But having fulfilling and intimate sex takes time!

How has porn set you up for unrealistic expectations for marriage or with your body image?

How has watching porn performers impacted your own self-esteem and identity as a woman?

How has watching porn hurt your relationship with God?

You might believe: *I'm not hurting anyone by looking at porn.*

Genesis 1:27 says, "So God created mankind in his own image, in the image of God he created them; male and female he created them." Every single human, man and woman, is made in the image of God and literally breathed into life from the breath of life from God (Gen. 2:7).

One of the reasons watching porn is problematic is because when we do, we are watching the abuse of God's image bearers, and we are using other image bearers for our own sexual gratification.

The average porn consumer has no idea what exactly goes into the production of a single pornographic image or video. You might not even think about how or why a performer got to be on camera or the situation that led them to their involvement with porn. You might not know that most of the performers do not appear on film under their own free will. In other words, you are likely watching victims of human sex trafficking.[2]

Not only are the performers forced to perform, but they may also be experiencing violent sexual acts. Eighty-eight percent of scenes in porn films contain acts of physical aggression, and 49 percent of scenes contain verbal aggression.[3]

Lusting, watching porn, or hooking up is the opposite of the apostle Paul's command to "do nothing out of selfish ambition or vain conceit. Rather, in humility value others above yourselves, not looking to your own interests but each of you to the interests of the others" (Phil. 2:3–4).

We covered some heavy topics today. Take a deep breath. Your freedom journey is no small matter. It sometimes means you must look at some difficult things, including the lies you've been believing. As you work through these lies, remember what you learned last week. God exposes lies not to shame us, but to bring us into His love and His truth.

What is one lie from today's study God is shedding light on in your heart?

Write a prayer to God asking for His truth to cover and uproot that lie.

The Four Biggies, Part 2

Today we will cover what is perhaps the most damaging and convincing lie Satan tells people. Believing this lie is the root of all sin and temptation.

SATAN'S BIG LIE #3 — YOU CAN'T TRUST GOD

Every day, as you make decisions for your life, you are faced with a choice. Do you trust what feels good to you, or do you trust God? Eve faced this choice as she debated whether or not to take a bite out of the forbidden fruit. As Eve sank her teeth into that piece of fruit, she chose to believe in her heart: *My way is better than God's way.*

Eve didn't invent this thought on her own. Let's take a look at how Satan suggested this mammoth lie.

"You will not certainly die," the serpent said to the woman. "For God knows that when you eat from it your eyes will be opened, and you will be like God, knowing good and evil." (Gen. 3:4-5)

Satan planted the thought that perhaps God was holding out on Eve. Rather than wanting what was good and right for His daughter, God was being vindictive, keeping the best for Himself. What happened next shows us that Eve fell for the lie:

When the woman saw that the fruit of the tree was good for food and pleasing to the eye, and also desirable for gaining wisdom, she took some and ate it. (Gen. 3:6a)

Let's make this personal. Have you ever wondered if God is keeping something good from you? There are times when sex and pornography are *pleasing to your eye* and *desirable.* Maybe you feel like you would be a naïve prude if you followed God's design for sex. Instead, you want to *gain the wisdom of the world* by sampling all that it offers.

Something that happened in a garden thousands of years ago is feeling close to home!

You might believe: *I know what I need better than God does.*

Emilee believed this lie too:

> When I'm at work and with friends, I don't think about porn. But during the evenings and lonely weekends, I feel like the walls start closing in. Anxiety. Sadness. Restlessness. I know God doesn't want me to act out sexually, but sometimes I do it out of anger toward Him. Why doesn't He bring me a husband? Why hasn't He taken away my pain? I know it's not true, but sometimes I feel like He's left me no other way to find comfort.

Do you hear Satan's whispers in these thoughts? Jesus told His disciples that life would be difficult. "In this world you will have trouble" (John 16:33). Unfortunately, loneliness, sadness, rejection, and loss are part of living in a broken world. But Jesus followed this bad news with the good news, "But take heart! I have overcome the world" (John 16:33). In another passage, Jesus invites you, "Come to me, all you who are weary and burdened, and I will give you rest" (Matt. 11:28).

Where do you think you will find the most comfort? Through watching porn, or running to Jesus? Satan will tell you time and time again that God's promises are empty. Don't believe him! You and I know from experience that in truth, the promises of porn and casual sex are empty. You are going through this book because you know this!

Ironically, Satan himself believed a version of this same lie that led to his downfall. He believed he was like God. What a huge lie! In fact, the Bible tells us that this is why Satan was cast out of heaven (Isa. 14:12–14).

The scary thing is we act like Satan when we believe that our plans are better than God's. Essentially, we want to *play* God because we think we can do a better job of running our lives. For example, I acted like Satan when I demanded God give me a husband. I thought I knew what I needed rather than trusting God for His provision. Satan wants us to think our plans are better than God's plans.

What ways in your life do you claim to be like God?

When are you tempted to doubt God's good intentions toward you?

How does doubting God's goodness increase your desire to look at porn or act out sexually?

Share about a time that you chose to trust God in your pain and loneliness.

You might believe: *I've tried so hard to experience freedom. God should have taken this away by now.*

We often feel angry at God for not taking away our pain and our struggle. In my healing journey, I would get frustrated thinking, "God just isn't working fast enough." As a result, I started believing the lie that I couldn't trust God with this part of my story. A few times these thoughts caused me to give up pursuing freedom and instead run after my sinful desires. Anger toward God has caused many Christians to walk away from church and from their faith.

Our emotions are real. It's okay to express our anger at God; He can handle it. We can be upset that we've struggled for so long. However, that is not the same thing as demanding God's healing in our own time instead of trusting in His timeline. Peter reminds us that ". . . with the Lord a day is like a thousand years, and a thousand years are like a day" (2 Peter 3:8). God sees the efforts you are making. He will bless you with freedom, but it may not happen when and how you would like.

Read Psalm 13. In what ways can you identify with David's frustration and cry in this psalm?

What did David choose (reflected in vv. 5–6)?

How can you make a similar choice in the middle of your frustration and questions?

SATAN'S BIG LIE #4 — YOU WILL NEVER BE WHOLE

Unfortunately, Satan's lies don't end once we've fallen into sin. Why? Because his endgame is not to get you to sin, but to cause you to feel distant from God's love. Let that sink in again. Satan's ultimate desire isn't to get you to look at porn, but to make you think you're too far gone to receive God's mercy, grace, and love.

Satan is called "the accuser." In fact, if you look all the way through the Bible to the last book called Revelation, you will read that Satan accuses God's people *day and night*. What Satan began in Genesis, he carried on through Revelation.

You might believe: *I'm damaged goods because of my sexual past.*

One time at a speaking event, I (Joy) met a woman who believed this very lie. After she heard me share my story, she timidly approached me. With tears in her eyes, hesitating to ask, she whispered, "Will my future husband still love and forgive me?" My new friend had a fear common to women who have found freedom from sexual sin — *Something is wrong with me.* Jesus freed her from the chains of pornography, but currently she was gripped by the chains of fear.

Did you know that in the books of Hosea and Isaiah, Israel is compared to a prostitute? Over and over again the Scriptures refer to God's people abandoning Him. Yet God, in His love and mercy, never stopped loving His people, no matter their past. God was able to forgive the past of a prostitute nation and see them as new, pure, forgiven, redeemed, and called.

If God gives you a husband who embraces you and loves you through your struggle, that is an amazing gift. A God-fearing man may be a shadow of God's love for you. But remember, no man is your healer. You don't need marriage to heal or to become whole.

On a scale of 1 to 10 (1, not at all; 10, a lot!), how much do you believe the lie that you're damaged goods because of your sexual past? How does this lie impact your life?

How can you find comfort in God's love for you, His child, to counteract the lie?

You might believe: *What I've done is beyond God's forgiveness.*

There is something about sexual sin that somehow feels unforgivable. That one-night stand. Experimenting with that friend in your dorm room. The abortion. At one level, your head knows that God forgives you, but your heart won't accept this truth. You think, *I don't deserve forgiveness.*

Instead of walking in freedom, you punish yourself. You cut. You purge. You sabotage healthy friendships. You nurture thoughts of shame. You might even run back to porn because you don't feel worthy of freedom. Without even realizing it, you may be trying to show God (and yourself) how sorry you are for your sin.

Nothing you have done is beyond God's redemptive power. God's full forgiveness is not for some other woman. It is for you.

Oh, my friend. How I wish I could look you in the eyes when I tell you this truth: nothing you have done is beyond God's redemptive power. God's full forgiveness is not for some other woman. *It is for you.*

129

You do God no favors by living in the shadow of your sin. In fact, you allow the enemy to have victory in your life by doing so. Today is the day to receive and accept the fullness of God's love and forgiveness. Your purity, your righteousness, and your beauty is because of Him.

What is something you have believed God could never forgive?

Do you think this thought is from God or from Satan? Why?

Read Psalm 103:12 and 1 John 1:9. What do these verses say about sin that you have confessed?

How might you be trying to prove to God that you are sorry instead of embracing His forgiveness?

Over the last two days you looked at the four big lies the enemy tries to get us to believe. We pray that you now will begin recognizing the lies during your struggle. Tomorrow, we will get practical and talk through how to begin breaking free from the chains of deceit.

Breaking Free from Lies

I (Juli) remember when I was in a season of deep discouragement and bondage. Despite all of my psychology degrees, I seriously could not find my footing. My thoughts and feelings were swirling in a torrent of confusion, rejection, and pain. A wise mentor gave me the advice I am now going to share with you.

Where there are lies, Satan has a stronghold. I began to ask the Lord to show me the deeply rooted lies that were keeping me in bondage. I made a list of four specific lies. One of them was this one:

I have deeply disappointed people I love. I am unworthy of love. I am a disappointment.

Lies usually tie into our deepest fears, and this one certainly did. One of my greatest fears was losing the love of someone close to me. In this season, I had experienced rejection from someone with whom I had a very deep and trusting relationship. I was devastated.

As I listed these core lies and identified my fears, I also sought God's Word for truth. Here's what you and I need to understand. The Bible isn't just one opinion or perspective to add to the others. It is *truth*. Truth is the only weapon we have to expose and defeat lies. Reading, memorizing, and meditating on God's Word retrains our minds from being entrenched in lies to walking in what is true.

When I (Juli) was in that season of deep depression and rejection, I memorized Psalm 103. At first, these words were just verses, but they slowly became my anchor of truth. I thought about the words at night when I couldn't sleep. I silently recited the words over and over as I wept. I personalized these words on my knees as I cried out to God. "As high as the heavens are above the earth, so great is your love *for me!* You will not hold my sin against me. You have compassion on me like a father has compassion on his child." God's Word became a weapon against the spiritual forces that discouraged and accused me. Through this psalm, I experienced the presence and truth of Jesus in my life.

REVISITING LIES AROUND SEXUALITY

This week we looked at different lies that are common to believe. Let's look again at the list together:

Satan's Big Lie #1—*You can't trust God's Word.*

God is okay with me looking at porn.

Sex is bad! My sexuality itself is shameful.

Satan's Big Lie #2—*Nothing bad will happen.*

Porn doesn't affect me.

I'm not hurting anyone by looking at porn.

Satan's big lie #3—*You can't trust God.*

I know what I need better than God does.

I've worked so hard to experience freedom. I've tried so hard. God should have taken this away by now.

Satan's Big Lie #4—*You will never be whole.*

I'm damaged goods because of my sexual past.

What I've done is beyond God's forgiveness.

In the list, underline the lies you resonate with most. (You can use these lies on the chart activity that follows.)

What could be some of the fears your core lies expose?

What would change in your life if you fully believed that God's Word is the truth needed to counter these lies?

Jesus said, "If you hold to my teaching, you are really my disciples. Then you will know the truth, and the truth will set you free" (John 8:31–32). Discovering the truth will set us free!

Now it's your turn to point out your lies and discover what verses you can begin memorizing. There is incredible power in identifying and naming the lies you believe.

In the chart below, write out a few of the lies you believe and then find Scripture to expose the lie. In the column on the left, write the lies—these could be lies that you read earlier this week or other ones not related to sexuality. In the column on the right, write the truth from Scripture.

The first chart is an example of the activity. Use the second chart to complete the activity on your own.

LIES YOU BELIEVE	TRUTH TO SET YOU FREE
God is not with me or near to me as I struggle with sexual sin.	Isaiah 41:10, Romans 5:8, 8:35-39
God doesn't care about me or my sexual sin issues.	Luke 12:27-28, Deuteronomy 3:22

LIES YOU BELIEVE	TRUTH TO SET YOU FREE

MAKING TRUTH PART OF YOUR THINKING

Read this account of Jesus being tempted in the wilderness and notice His weapon of choice:

> Then Jesus was led by the Spirit into the wilderness to be tempted by the devil. After fasting forty days and forty nights, he was hungry. The tempter came to him and said, "If you are the Son of God, tell these stones to become bread." Jesus answered, "It is written: 'Man does not live on bread alone, but on every word that comes from the mouth of God.'" (Matt. 4:1–4)

As a man, Jesus was the most powerful human to ever walk this planet, and what did He use to fight against Satan? God's Word. This shows us the power of Scripture. It's safe to assume that Jesus knew the content and significance of Scripture. And, He quoted God's Word to fight against Satan and temptation.

This shows us two things: God's Word has the power to remove Satan and temptations, and, to use this power, we need to memorize Scripture. Having key verses ready immediately arms us to fight when we are in battle. Most of us know that Scripture is powerful, but we fail to take the time to memorize it. (You could use an app to help you memorize verses.)

Choose one verse or passage to memorize from the chart you completed today. Start by writing it out here:

WEEK 5: SMALL GROUP DISCUSSION QUESTIONS

1. In the moments before watching porn or reading erotica, what are the thoughts and lies that play in your mind? For example:

   - What's the big deal? At least I'm not sleeping around.

   - I'm so good in every other area of life. This is just my one issue.

   - No one is going to know.

   - I deserve this. I've had a really tough week.

   - I'm unmarried. I'll stop when I get engaged.

2. How does acknowledging that these thoughts are lies help with your struggles?

3. Share the lies you believe and the Scripture you found to counter the lies on your chart from Day 4. If you were unable to find Scripture passages, brainstorm verse ideas together.

4. Believing lies are often the root issue to our problems. Believing one lie can create a chain reaction or snowball effect. How are the lies you just shared impacting your sexual strongholds?

5. What are practical ways to address lies when they enter your brain? (Turn back to your Toolbox for ideas.)

6. Satan wants us to think our plans are better than God's plans. He wants us to act like God. What ways in your life do you claim to be like God? Or in what ways do you feel the need to have control over an area of your life?

7. How does doubting God's goodness increase your desire to look at porn or act out sexually?

Stop Trying So Hard!

WEEK 6

When I (Joy) was in college, as a new believer, I had a lot of problems: no self-worth, emotional pain from sexual assault, and a sexual addiction. After confessing my pornography use, I wanted to know what to do to find freedom. Most Christians gave me the same advice: "Pray more and do more for God." Instead of helping, this advice made me feel worse. I did all the "right" things. I went to church. I prayed every day. I co-led a small group with my college ministry. Yet, I still felt stuck—I couldn't stop looking at porn. I figured, there must *really be something wrong with me!*

Maybe you can relate. You feel like a slave to your temptations, your failures, and your shame. You are trying so hard to pray, memorize Scripture, and say no, but find yourself discouraged by a struggle that won't go away.

This week, we are going to consider an approach to sin that you may have never heard before: Stop trying so hard!

Why You Can't Earn Freedom

In our Western world, we can achieve most things in life by trying hard. If you want to get in shape, change your exercise and eating habits. If you want to become a skilled musician, practice makes perfect! If you want a long list of letters behind your name, study, study, and study some more.

It's easy to apply this formula to finding freedom from sexual sin. You are going through this book because you want to *do something* to find freedom. That's a good thing! However, spiritual freedom never comes because of how hard we try.

God's grace, or unmerited favor, is perhaps the most difficult truth in the Christian life to really understand. To the core of our beings, we believe that people should get what they deserve. If we do good things, we deserve love and happiness. If we do bad things, we deserve punishment and sadness. And so we try harder to follow the rules and stay away from sin because we desperately need God's love and peace.

This was the trap I found myself in. I used to say to God, "Sorry I messed up, I won't do it again, God. I promise." Then I would eventually look at porn, yet again breaking my promise to God.

As many times as I promised God I would never again look at porn, I found myself falling back into sin. How could God still love me? I believed I deserved rejection and punishment because of my sin.

With this mindset, we do one of two things. We either stay stuck in what we believe we deserve (depression and hopelessness), or we work endlessly trying to prove to God and ourselves that we deserve something better (compulsion and worry).

Have you ever talked yourself out of happiness or enjoying a good gift from God because you didn't think you deserved it? You may even find yourself running back to porn again and again, because you feel like you don't deserve freedom. These may be unconscious ways of proving to God that you are sorry and trying to work your way out of shame.

What do you believe you deserve because of your sexual past or current struggles?

In what ways have you tried to punish yourself out of your shame?

In what ways have you tried to prove to God that you are cleaning up your act?

God has created a different path for freedom. It is called grace. Let me warn you, grace goes against every sense of fairness, justice, and pride in our hearts. God offers us what we do not deserve and cannot earn.

The book of Romans was written by Paul to the early church in Rome. This ancient letter explains God's grace and how it applies to you and me today. As long as you try to make up for your sin or try harder to please God, you will fail. God's path to freedom is completely different!

Read Romans 3:10–26. What does this passage say about every person's ability to earn righteousness on our own?

What does this passage say about what God did to make a way for us to be righteous?

Read Romans 6:23. What is the penalty for our sin?

What does God offer us through Jesus Christ?

Read Romans 8:1. What does this verse say about the guilt of those who have trusted in Jesus Christ?

Jesus Christ lived a perfect life, yet our lives fall far short of God's perfection. Because of this, Christ volunteered to bear the penalty for our shame in our place. He allowed Himself to experience the ultimate shame in this world—being stripped naked, being mocked and ridiculed without the ability to cover Himself for privacy, being beaten within an inch of His life and nailed to a cross. Crucifixions were reserved for the lowest members of society, and Jesus suffered that ultimate humiliation. He bore your shame and mine in His own body—that we might be free. But He did not stop there. He conquered death and shame, proving He was more powerful than either.

Are you getting this?

As one pastor put it, "We are not loved because we are worthy, we are worthy because we are loved."

HOW GRACE SETS YOU FREE

When we come to God with a broken and contrite heart, He doesn't turn away or despise us. God's grace in our lives meets our honest thoughts and feelings.

"My sacrifice, O God, is a broken spirit; a broken and contrite heart you, God, will not despise." (Ps. 51:17)

As you understand the depths of your sin and brokenness, let God's compassion flood into your heart. He will never reject you. He will never despise your offerings of a broken and contrite heart. As you learn more about your own brokenness, let this draw you into a deeper and deeper trust in your loving Creator.

Consider the stories of these two twenty-five-year-old women:

Jasmine grew up with a history of sexual struggle and pain. When she was ten years old, she gave her life to Jesus. Yet, through her teen years, she looked at porn almost every day. When she was twenty, she got pregnant after a hookup and had an abortion. Years later, she continues to struggle with regret and temptation. Jasmine's freedom journey is ongoing, even as a believer, yet God still loves her and pursues her.

Sarah got hooked on romance novels when she was fourteen. Her struggle quickly turned from erotica (soft porn) to hardcore porn. In college, she reached out to a friend and mentor who discipled her, helping her find freedom from looking at porn. She hasn't looked at it since.

Both Sarah and Jasmine have brought their sin to God and trusted in His love and forgiveness. Is one cleaner than the other? Does God love Sarah more because she more quickly experienced freedom from sexual sin? Does God love Jasmine less because she is still struggling? The answer is NO! God does not love and forgive based on our actions. He loves and forgives because of *His* character.

Maybe you have heard this message in church, but have you let it transform you? If you have never accepted God's gift of grace through salvation, you can make that decision today.

Here is a sample prayer for you. Saying the right words is not important, but rather the value is found in the passion of your heart. God knows our heart's desires.

Dear God, thank You for loving me. Thank You that Jesus died on the cross to pay the penalty for my sins and failures. I admit to You that I am a sinner, that I need You to save me. I ask You to forgive me for my sins. I turn from them now. I invite You, Jesus, into my life as my Savior and Lord. I turn my life over to You. I will live for You as long as I live. Thank You for giving me eternal life and making me a child of God. In Jesus' name, amen.

Maybe you have trusted in Jesus for your salvation, but you are still trying to earn His love. You can't believe God can still love you after all the times you have failed. Friend, both of us have been there. We know the struggle of trying to be good enough for God. Freedom comes when you let go and surrender. Will you lay down your efforts to make yourself clean and instead fall on the grace of God?

Confession: The Right Response to Grace

When I (Joy) first began to follow God, I continued to struggle with sexual sin and often went back to my old ways of looking at pornography. I began to hear this message about God's grace, and it honestly felt too good to be true. How could God still love me amid my sin and failure? I wondered: *Does God's forgiveness and grace mean that I will continue with sexual sin, just without the consequences and shame I once experienced?*

If you are asking this question, you are not alone. In fact, the very first Christians wrestled with trying to make sense of how God's grace impacts our behavior. In Day 1, you read in the book of Romans about God's incredible grace for you. You learned that there is nothing you can do to make yourself clean or earn God's love. He just loves you!

> *Jesus' transformation in your life does lead to a freedom journey.*

In that same letter to the early Roman church, Paul warned them not to use God's kindness and grace as a reason to keep on sinning: "What then? Shall we sin because we are not under the law but under grace? By no means!" (6:15).

God doesn't save us from our sin and shame only to keep us destined to forever return to it. In fact, Jesus repeatedly told the people He interacted with, "Go and sin no more." He healed them, loved them, redeemed them, and then told them to start walking in a different way of life. God does the same for you and me.

Jesus' transformation in your life *does* lead to a freedom journey.

One of the first steps in that journey is confession. Grace doesn't mean a casual attitude toward sin. Instead, it directs our hearts toward living out of a right relationship with God.

Confessing our sins includes three things:

1. Telling God what you have done wrong, without minimizing or making excuses.

2. Asking God for His grace and mercy, believing by faith that He does not hold your sin against you.

3. Expressing to God your heart's desire to live by His Spirit and depend on His strength to make you clean.

One of the most beautiful expressions of confession is David's prayer in Psalm 51. You may know the story behind it. David committed sins against Bathsheba and had her husband murdered to cover up his crime. He thought he had gotten away with it until the prophet Nathan confronted David with his sin.

In this gut-wrenching confession, David pours out his heart to God.

Read Psalm 51:1–17 out loud. List all the things David asks God to do for him through His grace and mercy.

What (if anything) does David himself do to become clean before God?

Confession is not only about what we have done wrong. It also includes understanding our inability to change ourselves. When I used to fall back into sin, I would say to God: "I'm so sorry I messed up! I won't do it again, God. I promise! I know I've said this countless times and have always broken my promise."

Have you ever felt discouraged by your failure to live up to God's standard? Do you promise to run from your sexual sin only to find yourself falling into it once again? Welcome to the Christian life. The apostle Paul experienced exactly the anguish we often encounter:

I don't really understand myself, for I want to do what is right, but I don't do it. Instead, I do what I hate . . . I have discovered this principle of life—that when I want to do what is right, I inevitably do what is wrong. I love God's law with all my heart. But there is another power within me that is at war with my mind. This power makes me a slave to the sin that is still within me. Oh, what a miserable person I am! Who will free me from this life that is dominated by sin and death? (Rom. 7:15, 21–24 NLT)

I (Juli) have lived much of my early Christian life with this great burden—wanting to do what is right but falling repeatedly into sin and hating myself for it. I had a relationship with God and understood that He forgives sin. So why didn't I feel free?

It may sound crazy, but I needed to stop trying so hard to be "good" and instead focus on surrender. I began to lay down my efforts of self-control and self-improvement and gave my life totally and completely to the work of God. I have one job; it is to surrender. This means I come before God empty and desperate, no longer trying to impress Him with my efforts of reform. When we say, "I promise," we are saying that in our own strength we will stop looking at porn. Even if we don't look at porn, we may lust or lie. We need God! We can't stop sinning on our own. Instead of promising God that we will change, true confession says, "I'm sorry, God. I can't do this on my own. I need your help!"

Hard work is usually motivated by fear. Surrender is motivated by love and gratitude.

Hard work is usually motivated by fear. Surrender is motivated by love and gratitude. Sin loses its hold on us only when we are captured by something more powerful.

I was recently talking with a close friend, Hannah, who has been a Christian for most of her life. She was sharing about a new level of intimacy and love for God. "Juli, why didn't I see this before? Why do all the Christians I know not have this joy? This freedom? This love for God? How are we missing this?"

I totally understood what she was asking. Satan doesn't just want to keep you stuck in a cycle of sexual sin and shame. His ultimate goal is to keep you so busy stomping out sin that you don't have the strength to run to God.

When we fall into Jesus' grace, we find that His love is so much greater than we ever imagined. His love begins to change our desires, shape our appetites, and heal our wounds. This is freedom!

Take some time with the Lord right now. Follow David's example by:

- Confessing your sin to the Lord

- Asking for God's grace and mercy, trusting Him to completely forgive and cleanse you from your sin

- Resolving to trust in God's strength and grace and not in your own promise to avoid sin

Becoming a New Person

The key to your freedom journey is found not in what you do, but in who you are becoming. When we place our trust in Christ, many Christians begin to immediately focus on how our behavior should be changing. Being a Christian often results in becoming hyperaware of what you should and should not be *doing*.

Here is a very important truth to digest: Christianity is not a change in what we *do*, but a transformation of who we *are*. Behavior and obedience are an important part of following Jesus, but they are the *fruit* of God's transformation in our hearts. You will not ultimately have the power to change your behaviors until you fully accept your new identity in Christ Jesus.

WHY BECOMING A NEW PERSON IS KEY

I (Juli) was born, raised, and currently live in Northeast Ohio. I have lived in other places over the years, but Akron is home. As we like to say in my city, "I'm just a girl from Akron." If you spend enough time with me, you will see evidence of this heritage—my Midwest accent, the fact that I call soda "pop," and my unwavering love for Cleveland sports.

This part of my identity flavors how I dress, how I talk, and how I interact with the world. Affections and attitudes will always be the result of identity. We *do* because we *are*.

All of us have different markers of identity, like ethnicity, age, gender, interests and hobbies. Each one of these influences and expresses who we are.

List a few of the identities that currently define you.

Give some examples of how each of these identities are expressed through your behavior and affections.

The invitation to know God through Jesus Christ is intended to be greater than every other identity. God's grace in your life didn't just erase your sin. It radically transformed who you are as a person. If you are a Christian, the most important passage in the Bible about your sex life is this one: "Therefore, if anyone is in Christ, the new creation has come: The old has gone, the new is here!" (2 Cor. 5:17).

God does not call you to simply integrate a Christian identity with every other defining marker, but to recognize Him as "Lord of All." Every other identity pales in comparison to the most important thing about you: you belong to the Lord, and He belongs to you.

What do you think it means to be a new creation in Jesus Christ?

What are some of the old things (like habits, affections, and thought patterns) that have passed away since you have given your life to God?

What are some of the new things (habits, affections, and thought patterns) that have become a part of your life since giving your life to God?

HOW KNOWING JESUS CHANGES YOUR SEX LIFE

God doesn't change *what we do* until He first and foremost changes *who we are*. I know so many Christians who strive to live by the biblical rules of sex without first stepping into the power of knowing Christ Jesus as Lord.

This was true of me (Joy) in high school. I didn't know God personally, and when I went to church and asked questions like, "How far is too far?" I was met with rules with no explanation of a relationship. I thought if I followed the rules surrounding my sexuality, God would love me. I didn't realize the reverse was true. The more I loved God, the more I would want to obey Him with my sexuality.

Your most powerful weapon against sexual shame, temptation, and sin is not a list of rules, but walking in your new identity through Jesus Christ. God changes our sex lives not by an external list of rules, but through an internal change of personhood.

Paul himself experienced this. For much of his life, he prided himself in being a zealous religious leader, steeped in the privilege of an impeccable Jewish heritage and training. Then one day, he encountered Jesus. In an instant, he was changed, but it took time for him to "flesh out" this new identity.

Read Philippians 3:4–14. What are some of the identities that Paul used to define himself by?

Look at verse 8. What fundamentally changed Paul's view of himself?

What does Paul say in this passage about being on a journey of transformation?

As you wrestle with sexual pain and struggles, consider this question: Is there any identity, good or bad, that trumps your Creator's love for you and His lordship in your life?

If knowing Jesus is truly the center point of your identity, you will begin to see and experience the world differently. This is why the Bible tells us that we will feel like aliens and have different affections than the world does. Following Jesus means surrendering everything, including the powerful messages that once defined your experiences.

How does knowing God change the way you view sexuality?

How does knowing God change the way you view your past sexual sin?

How does knowing God change the way you view what it means to be free?

God is not calling you to simply live a sexually *moral* life, but to grow in the maturity of what it means to be transformed by Him. Imagine your life as if it were a house divided into rooms. Some rooms—like the kitchen and living room—you are comfortable sharing with casual acquaintances. Other rooms like your bedroom or office are reserved for people who know you well. And then there are the hidden spaces—closets, the attic, the basement storage—where all the junk stays piled up and unexamined. Growing in your relationship with God means that you invite Him into every room. Over the course of your journey with Him, the Lord will ask for access into not only the public spaces of your life, but the secret, hidden, and personal places.

And so, yes, He is invited into your sexuality, into your wounds, into your shame, and into your struggles. This is how we begin to experience true freedom!

Experiencing a New Power

Imagine that Jesus could be with you all the time. At any moment, you could turn to Him to ask for help, advice, comfort, and encouragement. Imagine that you were always aware of His presence when you were tempted to look at porn. He would listen to you as you poured out your heart after a painful breakup. How would your life be different?

Do you want to know something really amazing? In a sense, you have Jesus with you at all times through the Holy Spirit. Jesus actually told His disciples that they would be better off with the Holy Spirit than they were with Him being right beside them in the living flesh!

Surrendering to God is not just about what we *stop trying to do in our own strength*. It is more importantly about inviting the power of God to our everyday reality. We experience God's power through the help of the Holy Spirit, God's very Spirit, living within us.

Today, we are going to look at four specific ways the Holy Spirit ministers to us with power.

THE HOLY SPIRIT CONNECTS US TO GOD IN THE MOST INTIMATE WAY POSSIBLE

When you give your life to Christ, the Holy Spirit actually lives inside of you at all times. Paul asked the believers in Corinth, "Do you not know that you are God's temple and that God's Spirit dwells in you?" (1 Cor. 3:16 ESV). God is living and dwelling in your body. You are actually a physical temple that carries God's presence!

Right now, you are connected to God in a very intimate way. I've heard people say, "But God doesn't feel close." Often this is because we "quench" the power of the Holy Spirit by not listening to Him. We fill our lives with noise and activity and don't take the time to ask Him for comfort and help.

When God doesn't feel close, remember, "He will never leave you nor forsake you" (Deut. 31:6). One friend shared with me that she often beat herself up for feeling far away from God, when in fact, her heart was longing for Him. She just couldn't see clearly that God was always near to her.

If you truly believed God has never left you nor forsaken you, how would that impact your freedom journey?

What does it feel like to know the Holy Spirit is dwelling inside of you? How does this impact your sexual struggle?

THE HOLY SPIRIT HELPS US KNOW HOW TO OBEY GOD

As Christians, God's desires live inside of us and help us find freedom. Through the prophet Ezekiel, God promised His people, "And I will put my Spirit in you and move you to follow my decrees and be careful to keep my laws" (Ezek. 36:27). This means that because of the Holy Spirit, you can desire to follow God with your sexuality. Scripture also explains this aspect of the Holy Spirit: "He will guide you into all the truth. He will not speak on his own; he will speak only what he hears, and he will tell you what is yet to come" (John 16:13).

As a high schooler, I (Joy) felt the Holy Spirit speak to me and say, "This isn't you." It wasn't an audible voice, but in my mind it was very clear. God was telling me that what I was doing was not His best for me. I was not obeying God with my sexuality. In the midst of sin, this voice caused me to stop in my tracks. I remember crying and saying, "God, I don't want to continue living like this, but I don't know what else to do!" I had the desire to follow God with my sexuality, but I didn't have the spiritual strength to change.

Even though the Holy Spirit is the one who plants righteous desires within us, these desires, just like a seed, can take time to grow and flourish within our hearts. And we need to nurture the growth of these new desires by filling our minds and hearts with truth.

Have you ever wanted to follow God with your sexuality, but did the exact opposite? How did this make you feel?

What are practical ways you can begin to nurture the new desires of the Holy Spirit by filling your mind and heart with truth?

There are times that sin struggles continue because we flirt with sin instead of doing exactly what the Holy Spirit tells us to do. When the Holy Spirit points out our sin, we need to act. Instead, we often try to compromise instead of surrendering. "Trying harder" is spending less time on social media because it triggers you to sin. Surrender is deleting your accounts.

Read Matthew 5:29–30. What does Jesus say about our attempts to compromise instead of total surrender?

Read Matthew 6:24 and James 4:4. What does God say about our attempts to follow Him halfway instead of full surrender?

How have you been tempted to negotiate with God instead of surrendering to Him?

What is God asking you to do that seems difficult to obey right now?

THE HOLY SPIRIT GIVES US HOPE AND PEACE DURING DIFFICULT TIMES AND HELPS US PRAY

As you learned earlier, it is common to be triggered by things that cause stress, grief, and pain. Porn seems to offer an easy escape from negative feelings.

Instead of turning to porn, God offers to comfort us through the Holy Spirit. Paul wrote, "The Spirit helps us in our weakness. We do not know what we ought to pray for, but the Spirit himself intercedes for us through wordless groans" (Rom. 8:26). The Spirit also gives us hope and peace as we are more surrendered to Him. "But the fruit of the Spirit is love, joy, peace, forbearance, kindness, goodness, faithfulness, gentleness and self-control. Against such things there is no law" (Gal. 5:22–23).

Has stress or sadness caused you to turn to porn to cope? If so, did it take away the stress or sadness? Maybe momentarily, but why do you think it wasn't lasting?

List the fruit of the Spirit from Galatians 5:22–23.

Why do you think Paul uses the metaphor of "fruit"? What does it take for natural fruit to grow on a tree? What does it take for spiritual fruit to grow?

To what extent do you currently experience the peace and joy of God living within you? What can you practically do to nourish these fruits to grow in your life?

THE SPIRIT ENABLES US TO BATTLE THE FLESH
BY GIVING US GOD'S POWER

The Bible teaches that there are two main powers that fight for dominance in our lives: our flesh and God's Spirit. When we are ruled by our flesh, we can't choose what is right. We might try hard to obey the law, but we end up frustrated, falling right back into sin. But when we are surrendered to God, His Spirit gives us the power to think and behave differently.

This is the power God gives you through the Holy Spirit: "For the Spirit God gave us does not make us timid, but gives us power, love and self-discipline" (2 Tim. 1:7).

The same powerful Spirit who raised Jesus from the dead lives within us. This power is the only way we will be able to battle the desires of our flesh.

The Holy Spirit is your lifeline to freedom—you are not fighting alone. You have the Spirit of God inside of you to give you the desire to follow Him and to give you the power to battle temptations. You will start to experience times of victory when you begin to realize that in the moments of temptation, you have the power of the Holy Spirit in you to walk a different path.

Read Romans 8:5–11. What does this passage say about the power of the Holy Spirit to overcome temptation and sin?

How can you begin to rely on the power of the Holy Spirit instead of your own strength?

Maybe this week's lesson has felt like a huge paradigm shift for you. For years, you have been striving and failing in a cycle of promises followed by discouragement. God's path for your freedom is not about trying harder. It's all about surrender . . . accepting His love, falling on His grace, embracing His perspective, living out of a new identity, and experiencing the power of God's Spirit bringing new life. As you grow in your walk with God, this will become a new reality for you.

Remember that freedom doesn't happen overnight. Neither does surrender. This is why our book is called *Her Freedom Journey*. We need to surrender daily, sometimes hourly, to God. We can hand over every longing and desire to God and ask for Him to fill us up with His love.

When I (Joy) was newly on my freedom journey and finally understood that I couldn't earn freedom by trying harder, I was so discouraged when I had fully surrendered to God only to fail a few days later. In that moment, I could have let shame keep me away from God, but instead I ran back to God, confessed my sin, and embraced His forgiveness. As you continue on your freedom journey, I pray you will be able to run back to God and allow Him to meet all your needs.

WEEK 6: SMALL GROUP DISCUSSION QUESTIONS

1. Right now in your recovery journey, do you feel burdened or hopeful? If burdened and weighed down, how can Christ give you hope?

2. If in the past you've tried to earn freedom on your own by doing more and trying harder yet you didn't find freedom, what do you think happened? Why didn't it work?

3. In Day 2 you practiced confession in three parts: confessing to the Lord your sin, asking for God's grace and mercy, and resolving to trust in God's strength and grace and not in your own promise to avoid sin. In your small group, share how that process went for you.

4. Share an example of how you have tried to negotiate with God or justify your behaviors instead of surrendering to Him.

5. How does knowing God change the way you view sexuality, your past sexual sin, and what it means to be "free"?

6. How does knowing that the Holy Spirit connects us to God in the most intimate way possible impact your relationship with God?

7. Do you believe that God's grace can run out for you? If so, how would your life look different if you truly believed that God's grace never runs out?

8. What is God asking you to surrender to Him that seems difficult to obey right now? What would surrender look like?

Getting Unstuck from Shame

Ever since I first experienced porn as a young girl, when my body felt tingles of sexual desire or I thought about questions about sex, I felt dirty and unlovable. I thought something was wrong with me because I had desires and questions. In reality, these were normal preteen feelings and thoughts that were unfortunately awakened early. Because I had no guidance to understand sexual desires, whenever these feelings entered my body and mind, I believed my body was betraying me. What I've described here is an example of sexual shame.

Patrick Carnes, a leading expert on sexual addiction, defines someone with sexual shame as "feeling profoundly ashamed for having sexual feelings and believing that a person is bad for having such feelings."[1] Sexual shame can also be defined as "a feeling of unworthiness in the sight of God or significant other due to a sexual thought, desire, behavior, experience, or abuse."[2]

This week we will look at specific ways that shame and sexuality overlap, including: shame for who you are, what you've done, and what's been done to you. The good news is that shame does not have the final word! Our hope is that by the end of the week you will begin to experience freedom from the glue of shame.

Sexual Shame and You

As a young adult, I (Joy) seemed to be more "sexual" than my friends. I was not married, yet I had more sexual desires, curiosities, and questions than any of my close peers (married and unmarried). I felt so different. I wondered, "Did God mess up when He created me? Did He make me too sexual?" Any time a thought or desire entered my mind or body, I tried to push it aside. Those thoughts and desires never went away. In fact, they became more intense. As a result, I felt shame for who I was.

I carried this shame with me into my dating relationships. I had just started dating a guy (my now husband) and we were out on a date. We were sitting on the grass by a lake, holding hands and talking. We had set our physical boundaries and in this moment we were following them. As a Christian dating couple, we longed to bring God glory in everything we did, including the way we loved each other physically.

Yet, at this moment, my body didn't care about my pure intentions. Our bodies were connected only by our hands, but my body began preparing for sex. Without breaking any boundaries, my body had made its own decision. My body wanted sex.

If you are acting in a God-honoring way and pursuing sexual integrity in your dating relationship, your body may still desire sex outside of marriage. This is normal. You are not weird or messed up. You are God's daughter, who was created as a sexual being.

As a Christian woman with sexual desires and urges, my body didn't know that I was trying to obey God with my sexuality. My body was just being a healthy sexual body with hormones and desires. With every sexual urge and desire, I felt more sexual shame.

Many things can make you experience sexual shame, like when . . .

- You feel unworthy of God's love because of your sexual brokenness.
- You have sexual desires or curiosities.

- You don't like your body. *(This is also called body shame.)*
- You were told in a shaming way to cover your body because it is a stumbling block to men.
- You've experienced unwanted sexual touch.
- You look at pornography or read erotica to cope with loneliness.
- You habitually masturbate as a form of comfort.
- You experience sexual desire for other women.
- You compare yourselves to others on social media.
- You grew up in family and culture that never talked about sex.

Can you relate to anything on the list above? Take a moment to look over that list. Circle the ones you can identify with.

I (Joy) have struggled with almost all of them.

- Shame lies to you, whispering that no one will ever love you.
- Shame makes you feel worthless. You begin to believe the lie that if anyone (including God) knew about your sins and secrets, they would no longer love you.
- Shame actively keeps you away from God, the One who is able to free you from shame.

These feelings trap you and make you fear that even if you reached out to God He would not help you because you are "damaged goods."

Sexual shame feels like glue, keeping you stuck in cycles of unwanted sexual behaviors. No matter how hard you try to break free, you find yourself stuck back where you started and believing that you will never escape this struggle. I've learned to distinguish between "This is what I'm experiencing" and "This is what I choose." I can't control the desires I experience, but I can choose how I steward them.

Describe a time when you felt shame for experiencing sexual desire.

In this situation, what is the difference between what you experienced and what you chose?

How can this distinction help you pursue sexual integrity without going down the road of shame?

THE BEGINNING OF SEXUAL SHAME

Let's look at where sexual shame started. In the beginning, God created man and woman in His image and He blessed them and said, "Be fruitful and increase in number" (Gen. 1:28). One of the first things God commanded Adam and Eve to do together was "have sex and reproduce." God saw the man and woman's sexual relationship and said "it was very good" (Gen. 1:31a).

My favorite verse in the story comes in the next chapter when we read a more detailed account of the creation of man and woman: "Adam and his wife were both naked, and they felt no shame" (Gen. 2:25). Adam and Eve fully knew and loved each other. They walked around naked and felt no shame. They took pleasure in one another.

This means that God created us as sexual beings to be naked and unashamed. You are not weird or abnormal for having sexual curiosities, desires, or questions—this is how you were created.

When sin entered the story, the man and the woman experienced shame for the first time. This is the moment they became sexually broken. Read what happens after they ate the fruit: "Then the eyes of both of them were opened, and they realized they were naked; so they sewed fig leaves together and made coverings for themselves" (Gen. 3:7).

Adam and Eve saw their nakedness and experienced shame. This shame caused them to want to cover themselves up so that the other person would no longer see their nakedness. Sexual shame makes you uncomfortable, making you want to hide from God and people. Shame is not just a consequence of what happened in the garden; the enemy still uses it as a weapon to separate us from others and from God.[3]

Read Genesis 3:6–10. Why did Adam and Eve physically hide from God?

Read Genesis 3:11–13. How did Adam and Eve emotionally hide from God?

Have you found yourself hiding your sexual struggles from others? What do you think keeps you hiding the truth?

What "fig leaves" are you hiding behind, attempting to cover your shame?

God knows that we need to hide! And yet, He still pursues us and wants a relationship with us. God calls us out of hiding. *Look back to Genesis 3:8–10 and read God's response to man and woman hiding.* God calls to them and says, "Where are you?" He knows where they are. Shame made Adam and Eve hide from God, but God wanted to see them. God does not leave you alone in your shame. He invites you to come out of hiding and into His light. He calls you from the darkness of shame and into His presence.

In our shame we want to hide and turn away from God and others, just like Adam and Eve. But God continues to pursue us. Not only did God pursue the man and woman, but He also graciously provided for them. *Read verse 21.* He made them clothes for them because He knew they could no longer bear the shame of their nakedness. Then He did something even more kind and amazing! He made another set of clothes for us.

Read Isaiah 61:10. What does this teach you about the new "clothing" God wants us to wear?

Read Revelation 7:9. What does this verse say about how God's children will be clothed in the future?

The Lord walked with Adam and Eve after they sinned and He walks with you today. God can heal you, comfort you, forgive you, and set you free. Instead of running *away* from Him, run *to* Him. Just like Adam and Eve (who tried to cover their shame with fig leaves after they had sinned), we run, hide, and find our own fig leaves. For some of us, this looks like turning to pornography, for others this looks like continuing a "friends with benefits" relationship. Whatever fig leaves you are trying to hide behind will not provide lasting healing or comfort.

Instead of isolating, healing comes when you move toward others. Sharing the most shameful parts of your story is scary (I get it!), but God made you for relationship. When you allow others into the deepest parts of your stories, the chains of shame will begin to fall off. (We'll talk about this more in Week 8.)

What would change in your freedom journey if you fully believed that you don't have to run and hide from God, and that God loves you for who you are?

Shame for What I've Done

One Friday in high school the bell rang signaling that the school day had ended. I (Joy) told my boyfriend to meet me at my house and park at the end of the street. I knew we had about an hour before my parents came home from work. That afternoon, I gave him my body in the hope of gaining his heart.

Two days later, I sat in the church pew wearing my Sunday best, acting the part of the "perfect Christian girl" with a secret I knew I couldn't tell anyone. Pretending to be someone I wasn't tore me apart. I was searching for my identity in the physical and emotional love of my boyfriend, and I felt empty and full of shame.

I believed that being a Christian meant living a good, moral, and perfect life, so I tried to be a "good Christian girl." I failed a lot. I made bad decisions because my heart was wounded and I needed a Savior.

One day on the way to school, I was walking in the parking lot with my atheist boyfriend, and he looked at me and said, "You're a bad Christian." Immediately, I started crying as I ran into school. He didn't believe in God, but somehow realized I wasn't living out my faith. He came to youth group with me and knew I called myself a Christian, yet I was not following God. I lacked an understanding of what it meant to be a Christian and what it meant to pursue sexual integrity as a Christian.

Sometimes, our moral decisions cause shame, but you can also feel ashamed for things you have little control over (unique aspects of your body or things your family members have done). Shame is so sneaky because we often can't sort through the nuance of what we actually feel ashamed about. In the situation I just shared with you, I felt some strange combination of guilt and shame. The Holy Spirit convicted me of my sexual sin. This was guilt. Yet I was sexually acting out because I thought my sexual desires made me worthless. This was sexual shame.

SHAME VS. GUILT

The first step to getting unstuck from shame involves diagnosing it. Is that horrible feeling in the pit of your stomach shame or guilt? While shame and guilt can *feel* the same, in reality they are *not* the same.

Psychological guilt is the emotion we *feel* associated with doing something wrong. We experience "true guilt" or godly conviction when we feel guilty for something we've done. True guilt is a very good thing, particularly when it leads us to confession and helps remind us to make wise and moral choices.

Sometimes we *feel* guilty when we are not actually guilty. This is called *false guilt*. A guy I dated in college pushed the physical boundaries of our relationship. When I repeatedly told him no, he got angry, broke up with me, and said some pretty mean things to and about me. Even though I did the right thing in that situation, I felt guilty. (See how confusing that can be?)

How would you explain the difference between true and false guilt?

Give an example of when you have experienced false guilt.

Give an example of when you have experienced true guilt.

While true guilt leads us to confession, shame takes that guilt to a whole new level. Guilt says, "I did something bad." Shame says, "I am the mistake or I am bad."[4]

For example, let's say that last night you binged on porn. You woke up this morning with a heavy weight on your heart remembering your choices from last night. Your guilt is alerting you that you have made a choice that is not consistent with God's will for you. You feel horrible for what you did.

True guilt says, "I chose to look at porn in my loneliness instead of turning to God. I know better, but I fell back into sin."

Guilt recognizes behavior. Shame settles in identity.

Your shame begins to say, "God could never love me. I am a rotten Christian. Maybe I'm not even a Christian if I keep falling into this same sin!"

Shame comes from a sense of "there being something wrong with me" or of "not being enough," and feeling powerless to change our condition or circumstances.[5]

> *Guilt recognizes behavior. Shame settles in identity.*

Shame is so difficult to diagnose and confront because sometimes it comes from the wrong choices we've made and the impact of our own sin. Shame only tells half the truth. While it may stem from true guilt, it morphs into crippling accusations and feelings of unworthiness.

How have you experienced shame around your sexual choices—not just guilt, knowing that you did something wrong, but shame, thinking you are too far gone for God to love and forgive?

How does knowing the difference between guilt and shame impact your freedom journey?

Here is a pathway that may be helpful in addressing your experience of guilt and shame. *In the righthand column, write your answer to each of the questions in the lefthand column.*

STEP 1: Write down the circumstances that led to you feeling guilt and shame.	
STEP 2: Looking at these circumstances. Did you do something morally wrong?	
STEP 3: What conclusions about your identity are you drawing because of this situation?	
STEP 4: What does God say about your answers in Step 3? Are they based on the truth of Jesus Christ, or based on lies?	

CHRIST AND YOUR SHAME

If you are a Christian, you have already confessed and admitted that you are a sinner. You have acknowledged that your natural desires will lead you away from God. But through the blood of Jesus, while you may still *do* things wrong, your identity has immediately changed from "sinner" to "saint."

As a young woman, I (Joy) not only felt guilty about looking at porn, I felt shameful for being a sexual sinner. God might be able to forgive me, but I didn't think He could ever make me clean again.

The apostle John wrote about what to do when we feel badly about our sin: "If we confess our sins, he [God] is faithful and just and will forgive us our sins and purify us from all unrighteousness" (1 John 1:9). After confessing our sins, we can live free from our guilt because of Jesus' death on the cross.

Satan will consistently remind you of your sins, not so that you confess and get right with God, but so that you will never feel worthy of His love. Until Jesus returns and binds up the great accuser forever, our enemy will use shame as a weapon to try to steal your identity and keep you from a relationship with God.

My friend Adaobi shared:

In Nigeria, where I am from, sexuality is rarely discussed in homes—except to warn against unwanted pregnancies. I knew that if I ever got pregnant, I'd be thrown out of the house. Growing up, I wanted to experience how it felt like to be loved. I started early, looking for someone or something to fill the emptiness in my heart. I had a boyfriend in high school and we went too far sexually, and soon everything broke apart. I was devastated. He had promised he wouldn't leave. I felt used and I was ashamed.[6]

The sexual shame Adaobi experienced caused her to doubt who she is in Christ— shame impacted her identity as a daughter of the King. When asked how she experienced freedom, she shared:

Understanding my identity in Christ as I gave my life to Him. I poured everything out to Him, He saved me, took everything away including my shame. I was so empty, so depressed. No light in my life, no joy, no hope for tomorrow, no dreams. I was living dead. But Christ came and took all of it away. He healed my poor and fragile heart. He healed my misery. He gave me hope and grace. That is why my life is nothing without Him.

There is hope for you. Christ died so that we might be saved from our sins and that includes whatever is making us feel unworthy and dirty. It may sound so unreal and too good to be true, but once you meet Jesus, He will take your sexual shame away.[7]

CONFRONTING YOUR SHAME

How do you escape the tight grasps of the shame that Satan, the accuser, brings? Like Adaobi, you begin by finding your identity in Christ and each day becoming more and more like Him.

Remember, having a relationship with God is not simply going to church. I didn't used to know the difference, and going to church even made me feel more ashamed.

Here is the good news we don't want you to miss: Jesus came to free you from shame. Because of Christ's death on the cross, those who trust in God will not endure shame from our Creator. The apostle Peter, who wept bitterly after he denied Jesus three times, wrote, "and the one who trusts in him will never be put to shame" (1 Peter 2:6). The phrase "never be put to shame" refers to the future. This verse promises Christians that we have an ultimate victory because of Christ. Guilt is a sin issue, but shame is an identity issue. We must understand our identity in Christ to live out freedom from shame.

You might still feel shame—but those feelings fail to match reality. Because we have Jesus as our Savior, Redeemer, and lover of our souls, we have freedom. All who become Christians have a new identity—declared righteous before God—in Christ. God has set us apart. Sin no longer has a hold on us and no longer defines our identity. Our new reality does not mean that we will not sin anymore, yet now our identity is in Christ. Sin no longer defines us or enslaves us. Everything has changed. You may not feel it, but that is the reality Christ purchased for you on the cross.

Read Romans 8:1. What do you think Paul meant when he wrote, "There is now no condemnation for those who are in Christ Jesus"?

How does it feel knowing that you have a new identity—declared righteous before God, set apart, and that sin no longer has a hold on you? Do you believe this is true about you? Why or why not?

How does knowing as a believer you will "never be put to shame" impact your freedom journey?

Shame for What's Been Done to You

*Trigger warning—today's devotional mentions stories of sexual abuse and assault.

Over half of women experience sexual violence during their lifetime, and these are just those who report it.[8] I (Joy) am one of them.

Sexual violence or exploitation involves an actual or attempted abuse of a position of vulnerability, power, or trust, for sexual purposes.[9] It can include date rape, sexual assault, unwanted sexual touch, coarse joking and harassment, child sexual abuse, or early exposure to pornography.

One of Satan's most powerful weapons is planting shame in the heart of our wounds. This happened to one woman who was molested at the age of eight and hid that secret for many years. The longer the pain went unchecked, the more the shame grew. In her shame, she turned to casual sex, which left her feeling more unworthy and experiencing more sexual brokenness.

Many women experience confusion between what has been done to them sexually and their sexual sin. They wonder, "Was it my fault?"

As a victim of sexual assault, I struggled with blaming myself for what happened to me. I wondered if at some level, it was my fault. Even though I had said no, I had gone to his apartment. This was the argument playing over and over in my head. It would take me years to fully believe that the rape was not my fault.

If you experienced sexual touch before you were old enough to give consent, that is abuse. If you were ever manipulated or coerced into sexual activity, what happened to you was wrong. Even if you felt physical pleasure or arousal from whatever was done—it was not your fault. If this is your story, I'm so sorry for the pain you've experienced. At some level, I understand the shame you've been living with.

After going through something traumatic, we can greatly benefit from seeking counseling and therapy to process our experience. A trauma-informed therapist is most helpful because traumatic memories are stored differently in our bodies and brain than other kinds of memories.

If unwanted sexual experiences are a part of your story, have you ever felt shame because of it? Have you ever shared this with anyone? If not, what is holding you back?

The morning after the sexual assault, I woke up, grabbed my stuff, and walked home. I remember thinking about God. Was He there? Did He let this happen? Was He mad at me? Why did this happen to me? That night, I felt completely broken and worthless. I believed God would never love me again. I hated my body. I hated myself. I now understand that I was experiencing deep sexual shame.

I'll never forget how I felt the first time I looked into the mirror after being date-raped. I stood there naked, alone, and ashamed. I recorded my thoughts in my journal:

God, do You care?
God, were You there?
Were You there when her world fell apart?
When he took her identity?
When he took her hope and threw it on the ground?
How did You let that happen?
Why didn't You stop it?
This little girl.
The one You made in your image. Remember her?
Remember the promises You gave her?
To protect her. To provide for her.
Did You forget about her?
Then she looked in the mirror.
Naked.

Hurting.
Empty.
Garbage.
Used.
Abused.
That's what she saw.

Years have passed since that day, but that moment in time when I stood in front of that mirror will always be fresh in my mind. I didn't know it then, but through my story, God opened my eyes to His life-changing love.

In the Bible, we read a story of a woman who was also taken advantage of. Her story is recorded in 2 Samuel 11–12. We read about king David, who was supposed to go off to war but decided to remain in Jerusalem. Read what happens:

> One evening David got up from his bed and walked around on the roof of the palace. From the roof he saw a woman bathing. The woman was very beautiful, and David sent someone to find out about her. The man said, "She is Bathsheba, the daughter of Eliam and the wife of Uriah the Hittite." Then David sent messengers to get her. She came to him, and he slept with her. (Now she was purifying herself from her monthly uncleanness.) Then she went back home. The woman conceived and sent word to David, saying, "I am pregnant." (2 Sam. 11:2–5)

This woman was minding her own business and bathing from her monthly cycle when multiple men came to take her to the king. Here we see a power difference—no one can say no to the king. Bathsheba was a victim without a voice. She was taken to him, he violated her, and then she was sent back home only to later discover she was pregnant.

Bathsheba is sometimes wrongly classified as a "bad girl." You don't meet a lot of women named Bathsheba! In reality, her shame came through the actions of David. Yet, I'm sure she still faced accusations and even her own doubts like, "If only I wasn't bathing at that time!"

Imagine going through sexual trauma only to discover you're pregnant with a baby that is not your husband's. Then David tried to fix the problem by trying to get Bathsheba's husband, Uriah, to sleep with his wife. When that didn't work, David decided to have him killed. First the sexual trauma, then the pregnancy, and now the death of her husband.

Sadly, the story gets even worse. After David takes her as his wife, Bathsheba gave birth to their son, who became ill and died. Throughout her life, Bathsheba had to deal with the fallout from David's sin. The blessing came when she later gave birth to a son named Solomon, who would one day become king. Through it all, God had an even bigger plan for her story. In Matthew 1:6, she is listed in the genealogy of Christ as "Uriah's wife."

Put yourself in Bathsheba's shoes. How do you think she felt having been taken advantage of and then grieving the death of her husband and child?

How have events that have happened to you caused you to believe lies about your worth and value?

In what ways have those lies and shame made your struggle with pornography more difficult?

From 0–100 percent, how much do you believe that you're not defined by the abuse you've experienced?

Imagine how your life would look if you truly believed that you were defined by how much God loves you and not by life's circumstances. Describe how your life would change.

Bathsheba lived in a different time than ours. Most importantly, she lived before the birth, death, and resurrection of Jesus Christ who would be one of her great, great, great . . . grandchildren. I wonder if Bathsheba ever felt free from shame. If she were alive today, she would not only know the freedom of her infinite worth in God, but would be amazed at how God redeemed her own very personal story.

While your life will probably not be recorded for generations to come (like Bathsheba's), God is still in the business of redemption. I know because I've experienced it.

In my journal entry, following my rape, I continued writing:

But God, He saw something else.
He hadn't forgotten His daughter.
His child.
In God's eyes, she was as beautiful as ever before.
She looked into the mirror.
God looked out of the mirror.
God whispered into her ear that He was there.
He had been there the whole time.
He held her hand.
He comforted her heart.
He cried.
He paced.
He was angry. Furious.
His heart broke as He watched His little girl hurt from the sin of the world.
God's precious daughter, don't lose hope.
God was there with you and with you He will always be.

Think about the image of God portrayed above. If you've experienced unwanted sexual behavior, picture His anger toward your situation. How does picturing God like this make you feel?

Shame Doesn't Have the Final Word

This week, we have looked at different sources of shame. Maybe you are beginning to understand your own experience of shame, whether it is rooted in what you've done, who you are, or what's been done to you. For many women, it's some combination of all three. Satan doesn't care what he uses to take you down. He just wants to keep you in bondage to your shame.

Friend, no matter what you've done or what you're currently struggling with, shame doesn't have the final word. Today we will look at a story of a woman who lived a sinful life, yet shame didn't win. Jesus spoke forgiveness over her and set her free.

When we read the Bible, we see practical teaching like some of the Bible verses we've shared with you earlier this week. God is gracious to also give us a history of real people whose lives were impacted by the reality of the truths of God's grace, forgiveness, and mercy. One woman had shame written all over her. We don't know her name, but we know what people thought about her. Her story is found in Luke.

Read how we are introduced to her in Luke 7:36–50.

This woman was known throughout her community as a sinner. Talk about shame! While we don't know the details, it is reasonable to assume that she experienced the trifecta of shame: shame for who she was, shame for what she had done, and very likely shame for what had been done to her. Yet, she has the audacity and the courage to arrive uninvited to a dinner for Jesus hosted by the elite religious leaders. Think about that for a moment. Imagine that a woman known to be a porn star crashed a meeting with the greatest Christian leaders of our day.

Look back at Luke 7:40–50 to find out what happens.

By Jesus' response, we see that this woman had experienced true guilt and godly conviction. In fact, He said, "her *many* sins have been forgiven" (Luke 7:47). Her heart was broken with remorse, and that sadness led her to the feet of Jesus. What Jesus said to her and about her was and is transformational. He used her as an example to this stuffy religious leader of what true love and worship should look like. Do you see it? The one who was undone by her sin and shame in one minute became the teacher—the example of godliness. Jesus not only took away her sin, He changed her identity! In an instant, she went from being known as "the one who sinned much" to becoming "the one who loves much" (Luke 7:47).

So what does this have to do with you? This week's lesson may be stirring up in your memories, bringing to the surface the agonizing feelings of unworthiness, accusation, and brokenness. This woman who lived so long ago is proof that Jesus is waiting for you. He is waiting to forgive you and to speak a new identity over you.

The greater awareness for our sin, the greater awareness we have for our need for forgiveness. What sins have Jesus canceled and forgiven in your life?

How does your love for Him grow through seeing the need for your forgiveness?

To end this week, we want to encourage you to do three things:

1. Take a bold step toward Jesus

You don't have to crash a party with a bunch of pastors, but pursuing Jesus may require boldly believing that He wants to be with you. The voice of shame may feel as powerful as a crowd laughing at you and judging you. But Jesus says, "Come." Will you fall on your knees right here and now to meet Jesus?

2. Worship Him

This woman became known as one who loves because of how she worshiped. In her sorrow and need, she didn't focus on her sin, but on her Savior. Jesus' physical feet are not here on earth for you to wash, but worshiping Him can be just as real. Give Him your tears. Tell Him how much you love Him and need Him.

3. Walk by faith

Friend, please notice that this woman's surroundings didn't change. Her past didn't magically disappear. She still had to live among people who most likely reminded her of her sin and shame. She still had to battle the lies within her own thoughts, convincing her of her unworthiness. To "go in peace," she had to believe that the truth of Jesus was greater than the voices around her or within her. How about you?

I will start a prayer for you below, but feel free to add on to make it your own:

Dear God,
I come to You today on my knees in prayer and I seek You for forgiveness.
Thank You for loving me even when I feel unlovable.
Thank You for. . .
I confess that I've fallen short and need You to make me righteous.
I confess. . .
I need Your power to make me whole.
I need Your. . .
Help me to live in peace.
Help me to. . .
I love You.

WEEK 7: SMALL GROUP DISCUSSION QUESTIONS

1. In your own words, explain the difference between guilt and shame. How does knowing the difference between guilt and shame impact your freedom journey?

2. In what ways have you felt sexual shame for who you are, what you've done, or what's been done to you?

3. What would change in your freedom journey if you fully believed that you don't have to run and hide from God, and that God loves you for who you are?

4. What "fig leaves" are you hiding behind, attempting to cover your shame? How does hiding make you feel?

5. Has shame ever kept you away from Christian community? If so, how could your life be different if you pursued relationships even amid shame?

6. How have events that happened to you caused you to believe lies about your worth and value?

7. In what ways have those lies and shame made your struggle with pornography more difficult?

8. Thinking back to the story of the woman in Luke, what does it mean for you personally to be transformed from an identity of sinner to the identity of the one who loves, just like she was forgiven and transformed?

When Your Story Becomes a Weapon

Since childhood, I (Juli) have heard that I was made "in the image of God." This one truth sets all humanity apart from every other created being. As image bearers, men and women have a special relationship with God and purpose in life. It is a great theological truth but sometimes doesn't seem to make a difference in how I view my life. If everyone is created in the image of God, then how can each one of us matter?

I was missing the truth that each man and woman *uniquely* bears God's image. As people we share some universal qualities of God, like we have a will, we will live eternally, and we have the capacity for moral reasoning. However, we also have the potential to uniquely represent the character of God.

Think for a moment of three people who have profoundly impacted your life. As I reflect on the three people on my list, one of them has taught me about God's unending mercy and love. Another has shown me the truth of greatness in being a servant. The third has taught me the value of a life of seeking God's wisdom. They could never replace each other because each has uniquely impacted my understanding of God.

No two people have the same story of God's goodness or exemplify the same quality of His character. We each have the potential to testify uniquely of the Lord to those who observe us or know us.

This means that no one can tell the same story of God that you were designed to tell. Think of all of the men and women chronicled throughout the pages of Scripture. David, Abraham, Daniel, Mary, Paul… Each one's life teaches us something special about the Lord. Their lives were not interchangeable but used by God in a very specific time for a very particular purpose. The same is true of your life. God has placed you here on earth to tell a very specific story that only you can tell. My question to you is, are you telling it? If you don't tell your story, no one else can.

If God is glorified when our stories declare His character, this means that our enemy, Satan, would love to prevent that from happening. He may have convinced you that your life and your story don't really matter. Or that because your story is "messy," you shouldn't tell it. Or he may encourage you to tell your story so that you are the star, stealing the glory from the One it was meant to exalt. Just as with the characters in the Bible, your story isn't ultimately about you. The story of your life was intended to declare the glory of God to all who know you.

This week we will look at how God can use your story to uniquely tell others about Him. We will also explore how telling your story is a part of healing and help you write your story. You will see how taking a small step of obedience can do more than you can hope or imagine!

How Your Story Becomes a Weapon

Throughout our time together, you have learned about the spiritual battle around your sexuality. Do you ever feel like Satan is winning? In some ways, we are outmatched by the spiritual forces that are more powerful than we are.

Not only can God defeat Satan's tactics against you, He also invites you into the victory. In the last book of the Bible, Revelation, we get a glimpse of the invisible spiritual battle. At the end of time, we see what is going to happen.

Take a moment to read Revelation 12:10–11.

Throughout this book, I (Joy) have shared repeatedly about how Jesus set me free. Remember the conversation I had with Zack about being freedom girl? In that moment, I decided my identity was not going to be in my sin struggle as porn girl, but rather in the power of my victory as freedom girl.

Since that time, I've been able to witness God using my testimony as a powerful weapon against the enemy, and God has used it to bring Him glory. He has brought many women to me who have similar stories, and He has used my testimony to help these women find power in their stories. God has used my story to impact women for eternity!

Our stories have power. Look back at the first part of verse 11: "They triumphed over him by the blood of the Lamb *and* by the word of their testimony."

Today, we are going to look at three important elements that turn your story into a weapon against your accuser.

THE BLOOD OF THE LAMB

The most important factor in turning your story into a weapon is the blood of the Lamb of God. Without Jesus' death and resurrection, there is no redemption! We triumph over Satan's accusations not because we are good or because we have said no to porn. We triumph only because we have said *Yes!* to the gift of Jesus' blood that covers our sin.

You are not the star of your story. Your story is ultimately about God.

This means that you are not the star of your story. Your story is ultimately about God.

As a human being, the most natural thing is to assume your story is about you, and God is simply a supporting character in your drama. While this is a normal assumption, it is also a false one. God cares deeply about you, but your journey is about Him.

Why is it so important that God becomes the main character in your personal story?

How has the "blood of the Lamb" changed your story?

Look again at the verb "triumphed" in Revelation 12:11. Notice the word is past tense, meaning that this triumph is a completed action. Jesus has already defeated Satan through His death and resurrection. When you become a Christian, because of the sacrifice of the blood of the Lamb, Satan is defeated. Even though Christ has not yet returned, we have victory over Satan's accusations.

THE POWER OF YOUR TESTIMONY

As believers, we know that Jesus' death on the cross sets us free from Satan, but did you also know that your story is powerful? It is—because Jesus' sacrifice gives each one of us a powerful testimony!

God can and will make a beautiful thing out of all your pain and suffering. Never let Satan convince you that your story has no purpose. Never let him convince you that your story is too shameful to share with others. Allow God to use your story to bring Him glory.

On a scale of 1 to 10, how hard is it to believe that your story has the power to triumph over the enemy?

If you truly believed in the power of your testimony, how would this impact your freedom journey?

GIVING UP YOUR LIFE

This specific verse in Revelation is referring to the martyrs who literally give their lives during the end times for the sake of Christ. Even though you and I may not be in a place to physically die because of our faith in God, we are all asked to lay down our lives in response to what God has done for us. Jesus told His disciples, "Whoever wants to be my disciple must deny themselves and take up their cross and follow me. For whoever wants to save their life will lose it, but whoever loses their life for me will find it" (Matt. 16:24–25).

How does this specifically apply to the power of your testimony? Sometimes telling your story faithfully requires the painful process of dying to self. To tell your story truthfully, you will need to acknowledge and possibly share some embarrassing and vulnerable aspects of your life.

I (Juli) have learned over decades of walking with God that one of the most difficult things for me to surrender is my reputation—what other people think about me. It's not easy to write in a book, share on a podcast, or even tell a friend about things I've done or thought that paint me in a bad light. Yet, God will only be glorified through my story when I share it obediently and not just to make myself look better.

How might acknowledging or sharing parts of your story feel a bit like "dying to self"?

In what ways would "loving your own life" keep you from obediently and faithfully inviting God to use your story as a weapon?

Why We Tell Our Stories

The Bible is filled with examples of people who have powerful testimonies. In John 9:2–3, we read of a man who was born blind. When Jesus and His disciples saw the man, the disciples asked Jesus, "'Rabbi, who sinned, this man or his parents, that he was born blind?' 'Neither this man nor his parents sinned,' said Jesus, 'but this happened so that the works of God might be displayed in him.'"

After Jesus healed him, the man returned home and people started to ask him questions about Jesus. The Pharisees interrogated him about Jesus. The man told them, "Whether he is a sinner or not, I don't know. One thing I do know. I was blind but now I see!" (v. 25). The man didn't have all the answers to everyone's questions, but he knew he met Jesus and he was healed. We don't have to have all the answers to share our story—people can't argue with our stories. We can use them to point to Jesus and give others hope.

There are many reasons why you share pieces of your story with someone. Here are four important ones to consider. Knowing *why* you are sharing your story will help you discern *how* to share your story. Each of these four reasons for sharing are unique and call for a different type of "telling."

FOR YOUR OWN HEALING

While sharing your story can be a powerful resource for sharing the hope of Christ, doing so can also help you in your own healing. Jay Stringer, a therapist and author of the excellent book, *Unwanted*, bases his approach to counseling around his clients sharing their stories. He believes that by sharing the formative experiences of one's life, his clients can uncover why they exhibit unwanted sexual behavior. Stringer found a 22 percent reduction in heavy porn use among those who shared their stories with someone in a biblical community compared to those who had no one to talk to.[1] Sharing their story and being met with love was the key for healing.

Many of the things I've (Joy) shared with you over the past seven weeks are pieces of my story that I've been able to put together through telling it. When I was younger, I didn't understand the link between my sexual shame and my porn use. I also didn't connect the fact that I sought physical touch with men to make up for my feelings of unworthiness. It's only been over the years of processing my story with my counselor, with close friends, and in my prayer life that I've been able to understand how the pieces of my story fit together.

You may have experienced that happening as you are going through this book. Maybe you are starting to make connections, helping you understand *why* sex has become such a powerful force in your life.

When have you shared vulnerable parts of your story as part of your own healing journey?

How was this different from sharing your story with a casual friend?

TO BUILD INTIMACY

The only way to truly be known is to tell your story. Intimacy is what happens in a relationship when you don't feel like you have to hide or pretend to be someone you are not. If someone only knows the acceptable or pretty parts of you, they don't really know you. And if they don't really know you, they can't truly love you. This is why refusing to share your story with those with whom you desire a close relationship will keep your relationships at a surface level.

As you get to know other people, you may share more and more aspects of yourself that also make you vulnerable. There may come a time in a dating relationship or close friendship where you think it is important to share challenging and pivotal parts of your story. Again, this should be done only once trust has been established. Not all of your story should be shared with everyone, but you need a few trusted people who are on the journey with you, who know the parts of you that are the most difficult to share.

Imagine you shared your story with a safe friend and then felt fully known and fully loved. How would this impact your life?

How has keeping your secrets guarded kept your relationships more surface-level than they might otherwise be?

How has sharing your story deepened a relationship in the past?

FOR GOD'S GLORY

Every time you tell your story, you give honor and glory to God because you are giving Him the credit and acknowledging His work in your life. Your story is the story of how God rescued you from brokenness, saved you, redeemed you, and forgave you. Your story is a story of hope. It's your first-person account of how your life has changed.

Read 2 Corinthians 12:7–10. How is Christ's power made perfect in your weakness? In other words, how is Christ glorified in your story?

How can we delight in our weakness, like Paul says, "For when I am weak, then I am strong" (v. 10)?

FOR SOMEONE'S ENCOURAGEMENT

When I was nineteen years old and heard another Christian woman talk about her struggle with pornography, her history changed my future. As she courageously spoke about her freedom journey, I was invited to begin mine. No preacher, author, or evangelist's words could have been more powerful to me at that moment. The same may be true when you begin to tell your story.

Stories offer us the hope of a future we can't imagine for ourselves. We need stories to give us faith that God's healing, redemption, and freedom are not just theologically true but personally possible.

Latoya shares:

Over the past few years the Lord has convicted me more and more to the point where I cannot ignore it. Hearing other women's similar stories showed me that I was not alone and that my struggles with sexual sin do not disqualify me as a Christian. This may be a temptation I always have, but He has granted me so much strength to "flee from sexual immorality." I am so thankful to know that I am not alone and I am not unlovable or unworthy. If I had not heard other women's stories, I may not have ever confronted my struggles head on or had the courage and the confidence in Christ to share my struggles. My sin does not own me and there is so much freedom in Christ.[2]

Has another person's vulnerability and story recently encouraged you on your own journey? Write about it.

Which of the four reasons mentioned (for your healing, to build intimacy, for God's glory, or to encourage another person) is the greatest motivation for you right now to share your story? Why?

Knowing Your Story

You can't tell your story unless you know it. As obvious as that statement may sound, it's important to acknowledge this truth.

What do you mean I have to know my story? I lived it!

You can spend decades reacting to your own story and stumbling through without really *knowing* your story. Just because you lived through something doesn't mean you have insight or perspective on what you've experienced. Our stories take time to process. In some ways, before you tell your story to someone else, you need to be able to tell it to yourself.

Today you will begin writing out your story to share with a trusted and safe person, counselor, or in a small group.

> *Before you tell your story to someone else, you need to be able to tell it to yourself.*

PROMPTS TO HELP YOU UNDERSTAND YOUR STORY

To help you write your story, answer the questions below. While some of these prompts are general, feel free to weave in aspects of your struggle with your sexuality, pornography, or shame. As you work through each question, you are putting together the pieces of your unique and powerful testimony!

One encouragement before you begin: your story doesn't have to be wrapped up in a bow to be powerful. We are all on a freedom *journey*. Remember our marathon metaphor from earlier in this book? Your story may inspire those who just started the race or someone right next to you who may have just tripped. You can help pull them up and encourage them to keep going. I know when I had just started my healing journey, I would have loved to have someone a little further ahead of me to tell me, "Hey, keep going. It's worth it!"

How has your relationship with Jesus impacted your freedom journey?

How did you look to sexual sin to find security, comfort, or happiness? In what ways did these areas leave you longing for more?

What were the root issues or lies you believed about your sexual struggles? How did replacing them with God's truth help you find healing?

How do you see Jesus continue to meet you in your sexual brokenness?

How has your freedom journey progressed since you started this book?

Below is an example of how our friend Gee, who is also on a freedom journey, tells her story through the previous questions you just answered. Let Gee's testimony be an encouragement to you in how and why to share your story!

How has your relationship with Jesus impacted your freedom journey?

Before Jesus, I was incapable of picturing freedom. I didn't know who Jesus was or anything about a freedom journey. Jesus met me in my brokenness in the darkness that I had known my entire life. He showed me the freedom He offered and gently asked me to surrender at His feet, all the trauma I had endured including the sexual trauma that was hidden and filled with guilt and shame. I no longer live in shame and secrecy, and although I'll live in recovery for the rest of my days on earth, I know that when temptation happens, I can run to Him and ask for help.

How did you look to sexual sin to find security, comfort, or happiness? In what ways did these areas leave you longing for more?

I grew up in a family where porn, masturbation, and sex with "no-strings-attached" were encouraged as a way to find independence, comfort, and happiness. Masturbation was a massive part of my tween and teen years. I wanted to feel "happy" and forget the rejection and abandonment I faced daily. Shortly after I turned twenty, my then-boyfriend exposed me to porn.

After we broke up, I felt lost, lonely, and rejected. I looked to porn and masturbation to fill my broken parts and heal my mind, heart, and soul. Sometimes I cried for hours afterward because instead of feeling good, all it did was shed light on the void within my heart. It left me feeling more alone and abandoned than before. This habit became an addiction. No matter how much of it I had, I never felt satisfied, loved, or beautiful.

What were the root issues or lies you believed about your sexual struggles? How did replacing them with God's truth help you find healing?

My sexual struggles resulted from childhood trauma, the lies I believed from a young age, and the choices I made as an adult. My entire identity depended on sexual acts and choices. My beliefs about sex were distorted. The men that surrounded me while growing up sexualized women and spoke of them as objects or toys. I knew that men watched porn but had never heard of women doing so. Learning about God's design for sexuality and what His Word says about it changed my thinking and exposed the lies I believed. I realized that I wasn't at fault for what happened to me, that Jesus' heart hurt for me in those moments. Even after choosing not to follow Him for so many years, He was waiting for me with arms wide open. My heart is His, and His blood washes me.

How do you see Jesus continue to meet you in your sexual brokenness?
As I've grown in my faith, God has exposed more pieces of my sexual brokenness. The beauty is that as He does, I get to bring it to Him and learn something new about Him and His Word. It is like going to the doctor and expecting a prescription for medication but receiving the secret to complete healing instead. I know that I am loved and that perfection is not what He wants from me. Instead, Jesus continues to teach me to walk in humility and have a heart of compassion and forgiveness.

How has your freedom journey grown or changed since you started this book?
Years ago, I had the honor of going through this [book] in a pilot group. Since then, I've been on a freedom journey toward God's love and healing. My healing did not happen overnight, but this group was pivotal. During the group, I felt safe exposing my broken pieces. God moved in a way that I never expected. I've gained a community of women who, in one way or another, can relate to my story of sexual brokenness and therefore create a safe space for me to share my wins and losses without judgment. The more I heal, the stronger the passion in my heart for helping women becomes. My story no longer scares me. Instead, I use it to glorify His name, and by doing so, it helps me grow in my freedom journey.

What aspects of Gee's story most encourage you on your freedom journey?

What is the most difficult part of writing your own story?

Time to Tell Our Stories

I (Joy) remember so distinctly one of the first times I felt God leading me to surrender my story to Him. As I was preparing for a summer mission trip to Miami, I had spent time writing out my story and prayed that God would use it by bringing other women who had gone through similar experiences.

One day in Miami, I went on a walk with one of my new friends that I met on a mission trip. She was upset and felt weird inside because the Holy Spirit was telling her to share her deepest pain with me. She shared with me that she had been raped her freshman year of college; I was the first person she had told. God planned that we both would be in Miami that summer. We cried and talked together, and I began to understand that God would use my story to glorify Himself.

During our conversation, she started asking me questions like, "Why would a loving God allow this painful experience to happen?" I also asked this question after my sexual trauma. I was able to share that we may never know the answer to this question while on this earth. I encouraged her with this verse, "And we know that in all things God works for the good of those who love him, who have been called according to his purpose" (Rom. 8:28).

I didn't have to have the answers to her questions. I listened and encouraged her and then I shared my story of healing. God used my testimony in a powerful way! That summer I helped my friend begin a journey of healing. Later that week, I found out that five other girls on the trip had been sexually abused. I prayed for one girl, God gave me six.

Here is my favorite part of the story. After the summer ended, this friend felt called to speak about her experience with all the sororities on her campus. She went to each chapter meeting and shared what she had gone through, how God redeemed her, saved her, and how she is now experiencing real love in a relationship with God.

That year, my friend witnessed ninety-eight girls pray to give their lives to Christ! Ninety-eight girls who were living in darkness were set free from Satan's hold. My friend realized that God could take her story and use it to change the lives of women, even for eternity. She realized that her story was powerful.

No matter whether you became a Christian at a very young age or you became a Christian after a dramatic life event, your story matters. God brought you from death to life. God can and will use your story in a powerful way.

If we keep our testimonies to ourselves, we are limiting God's power from working in the lives of those around us. We are called to live as Christ's witnesses by telling how Christ has changed our lives.

Think of one person who needs to hear your story. Go out and tell them what God has done in your life. If you can't think of anyone, pray. Ask God to show you who needs to hear about His love.

What fears or emotions are holding you back from taking steps to sharing your story with others?

Second Timothy 1:8 states, "So do not be ashamed of the testimony about our Lord or of me his prisoner. Rather, join with me in suffering for the gospel, by the power of God."

Are you currently ashamed of your testimony, and if so, how is this preventing you from suffering for the gospel?

WHO YOU TELL YOUR STORY TO

Your story has many different versions, all of which can be true. As you learn to steward your story, you will find that you tell it differently depending on the "audience." As you share your story, you make decisions about how much detail to tell and what to emphasize.

If you are learning to share your freedom journey for the first time, here are some guidelines to keep in mind as you think through what to share.

Knowing who is safe

There is a good chance that at some point in your life, you shared something vulnerable with someone who didn't honor your story. Maybe your secret became a source of gossip through a friend's betrayed confidence. Or perhaps instead of compassion, you experienced judgment or condemnation. If this has happened to you, I'm so sorry. It makes sense that you would fear opening up again. As safe as we think a person might be for us to share our story with them, they are also broken and sinful people.

In one of His most famous sermons, Jesus shared this proverb: "Do not give dogs what is sacred; do not throw your pearls to pigs. If you do, they may trample them under their feet, and turn and tear you to pieces" (Matt. 7:6). Pretty ominous advice! Jesus is saying that there are some things so precious that we need to be careful about with whom we share them.

The vulnerable parts of your story need to be treated with care. They should not be shared on social media for everyone to comment on. Think and pray carefully before you share your story.

Here are a few qualities of people with whom it is safe to share:

- Someone who is also able to be vulnerable with you.
- Someone mature enough to understand and handle your story.
- Someone who talks about other people with respect (if your friend gossips about other people, she will probably gossip about you!).
- Someone you have some history with.

Even so, we need to eventually get to the place where we are confident in our identity in Christ, so that no matter how someone responds we will be okay. A negative response may still sting, but it won't be crushing. Pray and ask the Holy Spirit to guide you to a person to share with and how much to share. It's important that we create healthy boundaries.

Have you ever shared your story and were met with judgment from the other person? How did you respond?

Write down two people with whom you believe it is safe to share the more vulnerable parts of your story.

Knowing how to encourage

I (Juli) have a young friend who is walking through an eating disorder. One of the ways I can help her is to share parts of my story with her. I remember what it felt like as a teenager to have some of the same struggles, fears, and thoughts she is now experiencing. Paul told the early Christians to "comfort those in any trouble with the comfort we ourselves receive from God" (2 Cor. 1:4).

How does it feel to know that God can use your story to give hope and comfort to someone else?

When you share your story with people who are struggling, here are some helpful things to keep in mind:

Pray for wisdom in the moment. Usually, you don't have time to prepare how you will respond when you are talking to someone who is in need. In the moment, ask God to give you the wisdom to know what and how much to share with them.

It's about them, not you. Don't confuse ministry with therapy. If you are still at a place where you are nervous about someone judging you for what you share, you are probably not ready to tell that part of your story. Sharing your story with someone who is struggling should feel encouraging, but not cathartic. You are not sharing to "get it off your chest" (that's for your healing). Instead, you are sharing to give the other person hope.

Less is more. All the person usually needs to hear is that you can at some level understand their pain. Sharing a small piece of your story will often be more powerful in doing this than sharing all of your story.

Sharing your story publicly

There are other times, you may have the opportunity to share your story more publicly. Obviously, this has been true of me (Joy) as I've shared some of my most vulnerable secrets with whoever picks up this book! Here are a couple thoughts about when and how to share your story publicly:

Don't share your story publicly until you have first shared and processed it privately. In the beginning of my recovery process, I didn't have the perspective and wisdom to share my story in a way that would appropriately encourage other people. This might take months or even years to feel like you are ready. Rely on the wisdom of a trusted mentor or counselor to help you know when it's the right time to share.

Telling your story is not a "start to finish" 500-page recounting of your entire life. When you are sharing your story for the purpose of ministry, you may want to keep the details vague and instead focus on how God has impacted your life. After all, your story is meant to point to Him! In an earlier week, we studied the Samaritan woman at the well from the book of John. Her summary of her story in that passage was: "Come, see a man who told me everything I ever did. Could this be the Messiah?" (John 4:29). This very simple testimony sparked a revival!

No matter where you are in your freedom journey, you have a powerful story. God has taken you from death to life. Use your story to help others find freedom!

WEEK 8: SMALL GROUP DISCUSSION QUESTIONS

1. Take a few minutes to talk about how sharing parts of each other's stories during the group has encouraged you.

2. Share about a time when you've told someone a secret part of your story. What was their reaction and what was yours? Were you met with love or judgment?

3. On Day 3, you started writing out your story. How was that experience?

4. What are some "pieces" of your story that have started to fit together as you've begun to process your story?

5. How would you describe your view of sexual sin and struggles when you first started this book? How did your view change?

6. Share about an "Aha!" moment during group time or while reading the book that powerfully impacted you.

7. What are a few practical tools you gained from this book that you can take with you into daily life?

8. What is one next step in your freedom journey? Share your next step with your group.

A Final Note from Joy and Juli

We know that finishing this book took perseverance, courage, and vulnerability to keep going. We hope you feel encouraged knowing that you are not alone and beginning to find freedom in Christ. We pray you believe that God created you as a sexual being and that turning to Him is the best solution to your porn problem.

Let's talk about your freedom status. It's okay if you are still struggling. The many women you have read about in this book (including Joy) didn't find freedom after completing one book. They took many steps over many years toward the love of God and freedom from sin and shame. Remember, freedom is a process! If you've finished the book and you're still trying to figure all this out, that's okay. This may be only the beginning of your road to healing and recovery.

These temptations may feel unbearable, but have hope.

Jesus was fully God and fully man, and He was tempted in every way. We will be tempted for the rest of our lives. Right now, these temptations may feel unbearable, but have hope. Jesus said, "I have told you these things, so that in me you may have peace. In this world you will have trouble. But take heart! I have overcome the world" (John 16:33). Jesus has overcome the world! That is why we have hope. In your recovery journey, there will be hills and valleys. We encourage you to lean into your relationship with Jesus in the hills and the valleys.

As you wrap up this book, here are some questions to help you cement what God is teaching you on your freedom journey.

REFLECTION QUESTIONS

1. What did you find challenging/frustrating as you worked your way through this book? Did you resolve this issue? If so, how? If not, what steps will you take to resolve it?

2. What are a few ways you've developed or grown because of what you've learned?

3. What have you learned about God throughout these eight weeks?

4. What are a few practical tools you gained from this book that you can take with you into daily life?

5. Spend some time in prayer, thanking God for all He has done through this book and everything He will do. Remember this verse: "Be strong and courageous. Do not be afraid or terrified because of them, for the LORD your God goes with you; he will never leave you nor forsake you" (Deut. 31:6). Even when God feels far away, He has never left your side.

You might be wondering, now what? What's next? We want to provide some practical next steps for you to help process through everything you've learned.

NEXT STEPS

As you begin to think through what is next in your freedom journey, here are a few ideas for next steps:

Find community. Are you a part of a church? If not, look for a church and find a community group or Bible study to plug into! We cannot continue our freedom journey alone.

Find accountability. Remember early on when we talked about the value of having accountability friendships? If you haven't found one yet, pray about asking someone in your small group or someone at church to check in with you regularly to ask about your struggle.

Learn more about God's design for sexuality. Maybe you finished this book and you want to better understand what the Bible does say about sexuality. We highly encourage you to read the book *Rethinking Sexuality*.[3]

Find a counselor. Some of this book could have triggered you or brought up past things that you need to work through. That is okay! We encourage you to seek out counseling to begin processing through these painful memories.

Explore authenticintimacy.com. On our website, we have blogs, podcast episodes, online book studies, and other resources to help meet your needs! There is a resource for every topic of sexuality you could think of.

Most importantly, continue falling in love with Jesus. Remember the quote from Week 4: "Freedom is not the absence of something, it is the presence of someone." We encourage you to run toward Jesus, even in moments of temptation and sin and realize that His presence and grace in our lives is enough. Jesus is right there with you walking through the pain and suffering that you might be experiencing.

We are in this journey together! If you have a question about anything in this book, please send us an email at info@authenticintimacy.com. We would love to connect with you.

Acknowledgments

We are grateful to partner with the outstanding publishing team at Moody Publishers, specifically Judy Dunagan, Amanda Cleary Eastep, Ashley Torres, Connor Sterchi, and many others. We would like to thank the many women who forged with us through pilot groups, specifically Julia Mitchell, Tamara Milanovic, Beth Windeknecht, and Gee Torres. Through your feedback, you made this book better and encouraged us to continue.

On a personal note, we would like to thank our husbands, Mike and Zack. Thank you for your love and encouragement through the process of becoming free and writing about the freedom we have in Jesus Christ.

Notes

Week 1: The Problem of Porn

1. In 2022, the number of female visitors on one of the largest porn sites (purposefully unlisted here) was about 36 percent worldwide. This is a 4 percent proportional growth increase from 2021. More women are watching porn each year.

2. Joy Skarka, *Sexual Shame in Women and How to Experience Freedom* (Eugene, OR: Wipf & Stock Publishers, 2022), 69.

3. Skarka, *Sexual Shame*, 62.

4. Adapted from "Porn Is Not Your Biggest Problem," by Joy Skarka, Covenant Eyes, January 23, 2023, https://www.covenanteyes.com/2021/11/29/porn-is-not-your-biggest-problem/. Used with permission.

5. Laura DeCesaris, "How Different Exercises Affect Women's Hormones," Rupa Health, January 31, 2023, https://www.rupahealth.com/post/exercise-affects-on-womens-hormones.

6. Jay Stringer, *Unwanted: How Sexual Brokenness Reveals Our Way to Healing* (Carol Stream, IL: NavPress, 2018), 232.

7. Michael B. Robb and Supreet Mann, *Teens and Pornography* (San Francisco: Common Sense, 2023), 5, https://www.commonsensemedia.org/sites/default/files/research/report/2022-teens-and-pornography-final-web.pdf.

8. Robb and Mann, *Teens and Pornography*, 6.

9. We highly recommend the book *Hooked: The Brain Science on How Casual Sex Affects Human Development* or the website www.fightthenewdrug.com if you would like to learn more on the subject.

10. One fMRI neuroimaging research study has discovered a decrease in responsiveness to dopamine from becoming tolerant to graphic images because of porn addiction. Valerie Voon et al., "Neural Correlates of Sexual Cue Reactivity in Individuals with and without Compulsive Sexual Behaviours," *PLOS ONE* 9, no. 7 (July 2014): e102419, https://doi.org/10.1371/journal.pone.0102419.

11. Joe S. McIlhaney Jr. and Freda McKissic Bush, *Hooked: The Brain Science on How Casual Sex Affects Human Development* (Chicago: Moody, 2019), 144.

12. Eran Shor and Kimberly Seida, 'Harder and Harder'? Is Mainstream Pornography Becoming Increasingly Violent and Do Viewers Prefer Violent Content?," *The Journal of Sex Research 56*, no. 1 (April 2018): 16–28, https://doi.org/10.1080/00224499.2018.1451476.

13. One study found significant association between reported pornography hours per week and gray matter volume in the brain for those who compulsively use pornography. (Gray matter is associated with healthy functioning in the brain and is responsible for processing new information, emotions, and movement.) Simone Kühn and Jurgen Gallinat, "Brain Structure and Functional Connectivity Associated with Pornography Consumption: The Brain on Porn," *JAMA Psychiatry* 71, no. 7 (2014): 827–834, https://doi.org/10.1001/jamapsychiatry.2014.93.

14. Marnie C. Ferree, *No Stones: Women Redeemed from Sexual Addiction* (Downers Grove, IL: IVP Books, 2010), 72.

15. In the ancient world, relationships between men and women were very different than they are today. People died at younger ages and more frequently, so women were often left widowed and then remarried. Women were not able to initiate a divorce, so the men would have had to choose to leave their wives or would had to have died. This woman probably had experienced several unfortunate events to have had five husbands. See Lynn Cohick, "The Woman at the Well: Was the Samaritan Woman Really an Adultress?," in *Vindicating the Vixens: Revisiting Sexualized, Vilified, and Marginalized Women of the Bible*, ed. Sandra Glahn (Grand Rapids: Kregel, 2017), 250-251.

16. Ibid., 250.

17. Adapted from Joy Skarka's *Freedom from Porn for Women: 6-Day Devotional and Bible Reading Plan* (Dallas: Aspire Productions, 2021), Kindle.

Week 3: A New Vision for Sexual Wholeness

1. "My Freedom: Growth Track," Bayside Community Church, 2022, Bradenton, Florida, 5.

2. Interview with Doug Rosenau, *Java with Juli*, podcast audio, November 15, 2021, https://www.authenticintimacy.com/388-single-sexually-whole/.

Week 4: Pursuing Sexual Integrity

1. Adapted from "Porn Was My Sex Education," by Joy Skarka, Covenant Eyes, November 4, 2020, https://www.covenanteyes.com/2020/11/04/porn-was-my-sex-education-joy-skarkas-story/.

2. Marnie C. Ferree, *No Stones: Women Redeemed from Sexual Shame* (Downers Grove, IL: IVP Books, 2010), 202.

3. Ferree, *No Stones*, 202–203.

4. Joy Skarka, *Sexual Shame in Women and How to Experience Freedom* (Eugene, OR: Wipf & Stock Publishers, 2022), 132.

5. Rachel Gurevich, "Trying to Conceive: Increased Sex Drive During Ovulation," Verywell Family, September 17, 2020, https://www.verywellfamily.com/in-the-mood-you-may-be-ovulat ing-1960259.

6. George N. Collins and Andrew Adleman, *Breaking the Cycle: Free Yourself from Sex Addiction, Porn Obsession, and Shame* (Oakland, CA: New Harbinger Publications, 2011), 168.

Week 5: Ditching Lies and Embracing Truth

1. Parts of this story also appeared in Joy Skarka's book *Sexual Shame in Women and How to Experience Freedom* (Eugene, OR: Wipf & Stock Publishers, 2022), 64, 127–129.

2. Here are some stats: 4.5 million people are trapped or forced into sexual exploitation globally. Sex trafficking generates $99 billion annually. ("Profits and Poverty: The Economics of Forced Labour," *International Labour Organization* (May 20): 7 and 16.) Forty-nine percent of sexually exploited women said that porn scenes were filmed while they were being sold for sex. (Melissa Farley, "Renting an Organ for Ten Minutes: What Tricks Tell Us About Prostitution, Pornography, and Trafficking," *Pornography: Driving the Demand for International Sex Trafficking* (2007): 2, https://www.prostitutionresearch .com/FarleyRentinganOrgan11-06.pdf.) These may just be numbers, but real people are behind the numbers. Real people just like you and me.

3. Ana Bridges et al., "Aggression and Sexual Behavior in Bestselling Pornography Videos: A Content Analysis Update," *Violence Against Women* 10 (October 16, 2010): 1065–1085, https://doi.org/10.1177/1077801210382866.

Week 7: Getting Unstuck from Shame

1. Patrick Carnes, *Don't Call It Love: Recovery from Sexual Addiction* (New York: Bantam Books, 1991), 306.

2. Karen A. McClintock, *Shame-Less Lives, Grace-Full Congregations* (Herndon, VA: Alban Institute, 2012), 14.

3. Curt Thompson, *The Soul of Shame: Retelling the Stories We Believe About Ourselves* (Downers Grove, IL: IVP Books, 2015), 13.

4. Brené Brown, "Listening to Shame," March 2012 at a TED Conference, video, https://www.ted.com/talks/brene_brown_listening_to_shame.

5. Thompson, *The Soul of Shame*, 24.

6. Joy Skarka, *Sexual Shame in Women and How to Experience Freedom* (Eugene, OR: Wipf & Stock Publishers, 2022), 86, 149–151.

7. Ibid.

8. "Fast Facts: Preventing Sexual Violence," Centers for Disease Control and Prevention, June 22, 2022, https://www.cdc.gov/violenceprevention/sexualviolence/fastfact.html.

9. World Health Organization, https://www.who.int/docs/default-source/documents/ethics/sexual-exploitation-and-abuse-pamphlet-en.pdf?sfvrsn=409b4d89_2.

Week 8: When Your Story Becomes a Weapon

1. Jay Stringer, *Unwanted: How Sexual Brokenness Reveals Our Way to Healing* (Carol Stream, IL: NavPress, 2018), 207.

2. Joy Skarka, *Sexual Shame in Women and How to Experience Freedom* (Eugene, OR: Wipf & Stock Publishers, 2022), 94 and 170.

3. Juli Slattery, *Rethinking Sexuality: God's Design and Why It Matters* (Colorado Springs, CO: Multnomah, 2018).

AUTHENTIC INTIMACY

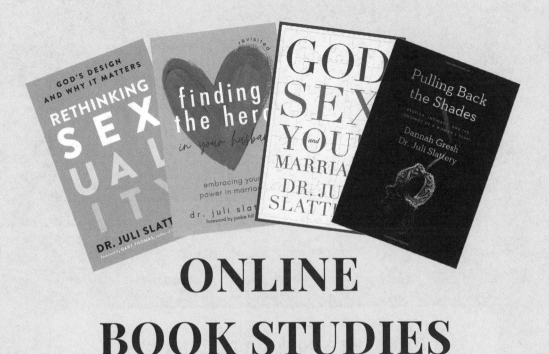

ONLINE
BOOK STUDIES

Finding community around sensitive topics like sexuality is hard. Online Book Studies help you dive into a deeper understanding of who God is and why He cares about your sexuality.

For women, men, couples, married, or single, scan the QR code to join a community of people also wanting to go deeper in their understanding of God's design for sexuality.

SEX AND THE SINGLE GIRL

A study on sex that goes beyond "just don't do it."

This is not a book simply offering a "don't do it" or "just wait" message—Sex and the Single Girl presents a broader understanding of what it means to honor God with our sexuality.

AUTHENTIC INTIMACY

Dr. Juli Slattery is breaking the silence

25 QUESTIONS YOU'RE AFRAID TO ASK ABOUT LOVE, SEX, AND INTIMACY

Find answers to your questions, liberation from your fears, and freedom to explore God's good gifts of love, sex, and intimacy.

Scan the QR code to grab a copy!

Java with Juli

WITH DR. JULI SLATTERY

The "Java with Juli" podcast features fresh, relevant and gospel-centered conversations about our sexuality. Dr. Juli Slattery dives into the "taboo" questions you're afraid to ask—or don't know who to ask—about intimacy, marriage, singleness, sexual addiction, and more. Every episode is an invitation to a biblical look at the good, the hard, the healing, and the holy in God's design for sexuality. Available wherever you get your podcasts. To learn more, visit AuthenticIntimacy.com.